W9-BCO-318

Bible Nurture and Reader Series

From a child thou hast known
The HOLY SCRIPTURES
which are able to make
thee wise unto salvation.

Rod and Staff Books

(Milestone Ministries)
800-761-0234 or 541-466-3231
www.RodandStaffBooks.com

Bible Nurture and Reader Series

Exploring With God

Teacher's Manual
Grade 4

Rod and Staff Publishers, Inc.
P.O. Box 3, Hwy. 172
Crockett, Kentucky 41413
Telephone (606) 522-4348

BIBLE NURTURE AND READER SERIES

"If you train your children carefully until they are seven years old, they are already three-quarters educated." This quote recognizes the importance of the critical early years in molding a child's life. The influences of childhood become powerful, lasting impressions.

The type of schoolbooks used certainly affects the developing appetites of our children for reading material. We will not instill in them appreciation for godly values by feeding them frivolous nonsense. We hold the Bible to be the highest guide for life and the best source of training for our children. The Bible reveals God and His will. Proverbs 9:10 says, "The fear of the Lord is the beginning of wisdom: and the knowledge of the holy is understanding." It is important that our children are exposed to truth from the beginning of their learning experience.

For the student to be exposed to the truth of God's Word only in textbooks is not sufficient to give him the very best. It is necessary for the tutor, be he parent or other teacher, to be firmly rooted in the Word of God and have the power of God's presence in his life. The Bible must be treasured as God's message to mankind. On that conviction this series is built, with the Scriptures as its very substance.

This book is designed as part of a series and will be most effective if so used. The seventy-five lessons of grade four are presented in three units with reader and workbook components. All the lessons are based on Bible stories or poetry.

Pupil's Reader	Reading Workbook Unit 1
	Reading Workbook Unit 2
Teacher's Manual	Reading Workbook Unit 3

Copyright, 1989

First edition, copyright 1969; revisions 1972, 1988

By Rod and Staff Publishers, Inc.
Crockett, Kentucky 41413

Printed in U. S. A.

ISBN 978-07399-0398-8

Catalog no. 11491.3

11   12   13   14   15   —   20   19   18   17   16   15   14   13   12   11

Table of Contents

A Word of Appreciation

It is with thanksgiving to God that we present these textbooks to those who are concerned about the spiritual welfare of their children. We believe that children are a heritage of the Lord and a sacred trust, and that we dare not fail them in any area of their lives.

The *Bible Nurture and Reader Series* is possible only because of the work and leading of God in the lives of many faithful servants of His. We think first of all of our parents, ministers, and teachers who had a concern for us and faithfully taught and nurtured us in the Word of God. We appreciate those who have had a vision of the need for textbooks based on the Bible and who have given their encouragement and help in the writing and publishing of these books.

We appreciate the work of the author, Sister Lela Birky, who has a deep burden for Bible-based school texts to nurture children in the fear of God.

We want to give recognition to the fact that we have used ideas from many textbooks, workbooks, reference books, and other sources. We are grateful for the work of many teachers who have developed and shared valuable helps for teaching this series. Sister Amy Herr is the writer of the present revision.

The Lord has provided strength in weakness, grace in trials, wisdom because we have none, joy in service, financial help, and faithful laborers in this work. May His Name receive honor and praise, and may we rejoice that we can be laborers together with Him.

Phonetic Symbols

/ā/ as in *pay*

/ē/ as in *see*

/ī/ as in *by*

/ō/ as in *go*

/ū/ as in *cube*

/o͞o/ as in *food*

/ou/ as in *out*

/oi/ as in *boy*

/ô/ as in *saw*

/ä/ as in *park*

/ė/ as in *her*

/ə/ the indefinite vowel sound heard in an unaccented syllable, representing any of the five vowels, as in *alone, listen, flexible, consider, suppose*

/a/ as in *hat*

/e/ as in *yes*

/i/ as in *sit*

/o/ as in *top*

/u/ as in *bug*

/oo/ as in *foot*

/sh/ as in *she*

/ch/ as in *chop*

/wh/ as in *when*

/th/ as in *thin*

/th/ as in *that*

/ng/ as in *sing*

/zh/ as in *measure*

To the Teacher

General Plan

Grade four of the *Bible Nurture and Reader Series* includes only seventy-five lessons. It is recommended that the students spend two days on each lesson. The first day with a lesson may be largely a self-study approach. Have the children read the lesson silently and do the vocabulary-related exercises in the workbook. They should then reread the story silently to apply any vocabulary knowledge they have gained, and to prepare for oral reading.

Allow class time the second day for oral reading and discussion of the concepts in the story. Include such angles of discussion that will help the students to do the comprehension exercises in the workbook.

If your schedule permits, you may want to check in class the workbook answers for the previous lesson the day the students begin a new lesson.

Workbook exercises which refer to the Bible are based on the King James Version.

Note: Students should be encouraged to ask about words that they cannot pronounce or do not understand. But a few words (especially in Unit 2) could be difficult to explain to them, such as *fornication* and *circumcision*. Help the students to pronounce such words, but do not attempt to explain the terms in detail. Rather, encourage the students to ask their parents about them at home.

Grading

It is beneficial for the students to check their answers in class. Discussion of any problem helps to develop understanding better than unexplained check marks. Seek to develop the students' ability to evaluate answers given with individual wording. The teacher's manual gives such answers with key words in italics. Have the students look for these key thoughts when judging individually worded answers.

Observation during this class session can provide you with a better awareness of the students' abilities than what mere figures can give. Express this evaluation in report card grades, along with written scores and oral reading performance. Occasional lessons recommended for written grades are noted in the Answer Key with *Gradebook* and the number of points in the lesson. Grades may also be recorded for some of the oral quizzes suggested in the teacher's manual.

Oral Reading

Oral reading should be taught and evaluated by giving attention to these specific aspects:

1. Correctness—reading the exact words that are on the page
2. Smoothness—grouping of words in meaningful phrases; proper speed
3. Inflection—conveying meaning with tone of voice
4. Volume—speaking loudly enough to be heard by an audience
5. Enunciation—pronouncing syllables clearly

Following the pointers given with the daily lesson plans should help accomplish the goal of effective oral reading. Use these suggestions with consideration to the needs of your class. Emphasize and practice the aspects in which they need help. The guide above can help you to include all the areas if you deviate from the pointers given day by day.

A suggested grading system for oral reading is to assign each of the five aspects a five-point range of value. Give a rating for each aspect according to the scale:

> 10—excellent
> 9—good
> 8—average
> 7—poor
> 6—deplorable

The total of accumulated points can be expressed as a percentage of fifty. In final grading, let the average of oral reading scores constitute one-fourth of the total grade, while comprehension and written work provide three-fourths of the grade.

Unit One

The Gospel of John

UNIT 1
General Plan

The twenty-two lessons of Unit 1 are stories from the Gospel of John.

Make full use of the map on the inside front cover of the workbook. Refer to it or a wall map whenever place names are mentioned. Locate this map area on the globe.

Type styles of the letters for the workbook sections identify different types of exercises. Bold, straight letters indicate vocabulary exercises suggested for the first day of the lesson. Italicized Roman letters indicate comprehension exercises that should follow oral reading and discussion. This pattern is flexible, allowing the teacher to vary assignments when desirable.

There is a unit test in the back of the pupil's workbook. The tests should be removed and filed before the workbooks are distributed to the pupils.

Unit 1 Lessons

LESSON 1

Introduction to John *and* Jesus Comes to Earth

Day 1—Vocabulary

Assign the students to silently read lesson 1. You may want to have them jot on paper a list of the words they encounter which they do not know. Then introduce the workbook. Point out the style of the letters that designate exercises A, B, C, and so on. Parts A, B, and C are intended to be done one day. Parts D, E, F and G are for the next day. Doing the vocabulary exercises should help the children with some of the problem words they may have encountered.

Discuss the directions for the vocabulary exercises to make sure the students understand them. After working these exercises, they should again read the story silently to prepare for good oral reading. If the children have listed any problem words which the vocabulary exercises do not cover, they should look up those words in the dictionary independently.

Day 2—Comprehension

Oral Reading

Conduct oral reading class. Establish some standard procedures to enhance order and efficiency. Begin with the following suggestions and adjust your method as experience directs for improvement or simply for variation.

"Stand with good posture to read. Stay free of any leaning posts such as a desk or wall. Hold the reader with both hands, one under the spine and the other on the open pages. Page by placing a finger on the top corner and pulling it toward you. Concentrate on reading correctly."

If a student mispronounces words or skips or adds words, have him reread the sentence. Give help as needed until he reads it correctly. The rest of the class should follow silently as one reads aloud. You may have each follow in turn to read a paragraph, or call names at random for turns.

Discussion

After oral reading discuss the story, asking questions on memory of details and events as well as discussing more thought-provoking questions of interpretation. Encourage the children to answer with complete sentences.

Suggested questions are given below. Deeper thought questions are marked with an asterisk. Ask such questions even though you may not expect the students to have the answers. Following the thought of your discussion will help them develop thinking skills in these areas.

Who are the Johns we read about in the New Testament?
[The New Testament tells of John the Baptist, John the son of Zebedee, John Mark, and John a relative of the high priest.]

Which one wrote the Gospel of John?

[John the son of Zebedee wrote the Gospel of John.]

What qualified him to do that work?

[John followed Jesus closely. He understood well the teachings of Jesus. The Holy Spirit gave him the words to write.]

Where was Jesus before He was born?

[Jesus was with God and had no beginning.]

How did God prepare the way for Jesus in the world?

[God sent John the Baptist to prepare the way for Jesus.]

*How were the Jews a chosen people?

[The Jews were given the Law and the knowledge of God in Old Testament times. The Jews were chosen for the lineage of Christ.]

*Is a Jew the only one who may be called a son of God?

[No, it is for all people who believe in Jesus.]

Who was born first, Jesus or John the Baptist?

[John the Baptist was born before Jesus.]

How could John the Baptist say Jesus was before he was?

[Jesus always was. He was with the Father in heaven before He became a baby.]

ANSWER KEY

A. 1. (zak•a•rī′ əs)
A priest at the time of Jesus' birth; the father of John the Baptist

2. (zeb′ e•dē)
A fisherman of Galilee; the father of the disciples James and John

B.
1. b	6. h
2. f	7. g
3. e	8. i
4. a	9. d
5. c	

C.
1. a	9. b
2. b	10. a
3. b	11. a
4. a	12. b
5. b	13. a
6. a	14. b
7. a	15. a
8. b	16. b

D. (The letter X should mark these numbers.) 1, 4, 7, 8, 10

E. (The letter X should mark these numbers.) 3, 4, 5, 7, 9, 10, 11

F.
1. after
2. after
3. before
4. when
5. after
6. before
7. before
8. when
9. when
10. when
11. When
12. before, after
13. before
14. after

G. (These numbers should be circled.) 2, 3, 4, 6, 8, 9

LESSON 2
John the Baptist Reveals Jesus

Day 1—Vocabulary

Check the students' workbooks for lesson 1 in class and discuss corrections. Assign lesson 2 to be read silently. The children should then do the vocabulary exercises in the workbook (parts A, B, and C) and reread the story.

Day 2—Comprehension

Oral Reading

Emphasize reading correctly. Do not accept substituted, added, or omitted words. If someone has a problem with such errors, have him slow down or read shorter passages until he reads exactly what is written.

Discussion

Why did some Jews think John the Baptist might be the Christ?
　[The Scriptures had prophecies that Jesus would come, and they were looking for Him. Then John came on the scene preaching and baptizing.]
How did the Jews try to find out if John was the Christ?
　[They sent priests and Levites to ask John who he was.]
*What made them think that John might be Elijah or "that prophet"?
　[The Scriptures also had prophecies about Elijah and another prophet who would come (Malachi 4:5; Deuteronomy 18:15, 18).]
Who did John say he was?
　[He called himself a voice preparing the way of the Lord. This was prophesied in Isaiah 40:3.]
*Would loosening a man's shoestrings be a highly honored service?
　[No, that was a lowly service, but Jesus is so great that John did not consider himself worthy to do even so lowly a thing for Him.]
How did John know that Jesus was the Christ?
　[John knew who Jesus was by God's sign of the Spirit like a dove descending from heaven to rest upon Jesus.]
Who brought Peter to Jesus?
　[Peter's brother Andrew brought him to Jesus.]
Who brought Nathanael to Jesus?
　[Philip brought Nathanael to Jesus.]
*What made Nathanael sure that Jesus is the Son of God?
　[Jesus knew Nathanael and saw into his heart, although they had not met before.]

Workbook Note

For interest's sake you may want to share the meaning of the complete names referred to in part C (5 and 6).
　　Elijah—God is Jehovah

Isaiah—Jah (Jehovah) has saved
Bethsaida—Fishing house

ANSWER KEY

A.
1. Scriptures
2. prophecies
3. wilderness
4. preferred
5. shoestrings
6. deceitful
7. ascending
8. descending

B.
answered
inquired
assured
questioned
replied
invited

C.
1. Levites, Israelites
2. Bethsaida, Nathanael, Nazareth
3. Cephas, Philip
4. Cephas
5. Elijah, Isaiah
6. Bethsaida

D.
1. "I am not the Christ."
2. "I am not."
3. "No."
4. "I am the voice of one crying in the wilderness, 'Make straight the way of the Lord,' as the prophet Isaiah said."
5. "I baptize with water, but there is One standing among you whom you do not know. He is the One who is coming after me, but is preferred before me. I am not worthy to loosen His shoestrings."

E.
1. no
2. no
3. yes
4. no
5. yes
6. yes

F.
1. The *Scriptures prophesied* of Jesus' coming.
2. John was *preaching and baptizing.*
3. They had to give an *answer to those who sent them.*
4. Jesus was *born* after John was born.
5. Jesus was *with God* before He was born.
6. John knew who Jesus was because God had told him that the One *on whom he saw the Spirit* come and remain was His Son. (or) *God revealed* it to him.

G.
1. John's home (West of the Dead Sea)
2. Bethabara (The lower name east of Jordan)
3. Nazareth (Southwest of the Sea of Galilee)
4. Bethsaida (Northeast shore of the Sea of Galilee)

LESSON 3
The Beginning of Jesus' Ministry

Day 1—Vocabulary

Check lesson 2 in the workbooks.

Assign the class to read lesson 3, do the vocabulary exercises for lesson 3, and then reread the lesson.

This routine procedure will not be repeated in the following lessons.

Day 2—Comprehension

Oral Reading

The words of a sentence are naturally grouped into thought units. Demonstrate this to the class by writing the following sentence on the chalkboard and reading it with pauses as indicated below.

It was the time that the Jews kept the Feast of the Passover at Jerusalem, and Jesus wanted to go to this feast.

"It was the . . . time that the Jews . . . kept the Feast of the . . . Passover at Jerusalem and Jesus . . . wanted to go to this feast.

"It was the time . . . that the Jews kept the Feast of the Passover . . . at Jerusalem . . . and Jesus wanted to go . . . to this feast."

Commas and other punctuation help us to know which words belong together in a phrase. Knowing the thought of the sentence also helps us to read it in a meaningful way. Encourage the children to think of the meaning of their sentences and read with phrases that express good thought units.

Discussion

Where was the wedding held?

[The wedding was at Cana in Galilee.]

What problem developed during the wedding feast?

[There was not enough wine.]

What were the waterpots usually used for?

[The waterpots were used to supply water for washing hands.]

*What is meant by the "ruler of the feast"?

[The ruler of the feast was a head waiter who looked after the needs of the guests.]

What effect did the miracle have on Jesus' disciples?

[They believed on Jesus.]

Why did Jesus go to Jerusalem?

[He wanted to go to the Feast of the Passover there.]

Why was Jesus disturbed about what He found at the temple?

[He did not like to see the business of buying and selling and changing money going on in the place of prayer.]

*Why did Jesus have greater authority than the Jewish leaders concerning what went on in the temple?

[Jesus is God's own Son.]

What temple would Jesus raise three days after it was destroyed?

[Jesus would raise the temple of His body three days after He was crucified.]

Workbook Note

Exercise A

Having the children write definitions may result in varying answers. You may count them correct, but it would be valuable to discuss differences of definition. Have the students recall the use of the word in the story and identify the best definition for that usage.

ANSWER KEY

A. (Possible answers)
1. The right or power to give commands or do one's will.
2. Top edge
3. Concerned about small details
4. Eager interest and effort

B.
1. whatever
2. nearby
3. into
4. Everyone
5. Passover
6. marketplace
7. policeman
8. understand
9. upset
10. without, anyone

C.
1. c
2. b
3. a
4. a
5. b
6. c
7. b
8. c
9. a
10. c
11. b
12. a

D.
4
3
1
5
2
7
8
10
9
6

E.
1. There were animals for people to buy for *sacrifices.*
2. People from *other countries* needed to have the right kind of money at the temple.
3. The Jews would *crucify* Jesus.
4. Jesus *rose from the dead* in three days.

F. Psalm 69:9

G.
1. from Capernaum to Jerusalem
2. northeast
3. south

H. (These numbers should be marked with *X*.) 2, 5, 6

LESSON 4
Jesus Explains the New Birth

Oral Reading

Write these sentences on the chalkboard and let the pupils draw lines to show where they would break the sentences into phrases.

"If I have told you earthly things and you do not believe, how shall you believe if I tell you heavenly things?"

"For God so loved the world, that He gave His only begotten Son, so that whoever believes in Him should not perish but have everlasting life."

For additional practice, you might consider the first sentence of each paragraph in the lesson. Call on individuals to demonstrate phrase grouping by reading these sentences with exaggerated pauses.

Emphasize smoothness as you conduct oral reading class.

Discussion

*Why do you think Nicodemus came to Jesus in the night?

[Some of the Jewish leaders were displeased about the authority Jesus showed. Perhaps Nicodemus wanted to have a discussion with Jesus that the others did not know about.]

*Why did Nicodemus have trouble understanding Jesus?

[Nicodemus was thinking about natural things, and Jesus was talking about spiritual things.]

*How is the Spirit of God like the wind?

[It is something you cannot see, and it is not understood by earthly wisdom.]

How does the story of Moses and the serpent help explain salvation through Jesus?

[Everyone who looked at the serpent on the pole was saved from death. Everyone who trusts in Jesus' death on the cross is saved from spiritual death.]

Childhood Innocence

Children at this age do not need to examine their lives for conviction of sin. The sinful nature is definitely there, but it is atoned for by Jesus' blood. Believing that Jesus saves them is a commendable, childlike faith. They can freely rejoice in the love of the Saviour.

Parents, not children, are responsible for the course little ones take. If a student whom you consider innocent seems concerned about being saved, assure him that Jesus' blood provides his salvation. His choice to yield to God will be important at a later time, when he is more responsible for his own life. Meanwhile, do not stifle expressions of willingness to please God. That is part of the praise God has perfected from the mouth of babes.

Communicate this spiritual interest to the parents.

ANSWER KEY

A.
1. d
2. c
3. a
4. g
5. e
6. h
7. b
8. f

B.
1. whoever
2. everyone
3. himself
4. everlasting
5. overlook
6. shoestring
7. bookworm
8. grasshopper
9. household
10. rattlesnake
11. treetop
12. furthermore
13. rowboat
14. driftwood
15. shipwreck
16. evergreen
17. headache
18. patchwork
19. cloakroom
20. suitcase

C.
1. f
2. j
3. a
4. h
5. c
6. b
7. i
8. g
9. d
10. e
11. o
12. q
13. s
14. l
15. t
16. m
17. k
18. p
19. n
20. r

D.
1. hoe, low, so, though
2. curl, girl, whirl
3. time, rhyme
4. glue, due, do, too
5. trough, off

E.
1. b
2. c
3. a
4. c
5. b
6. c

F.
1. Spirit (The others are men.)
2. Moses (The others name Jesus.)
3. old (The others relate to beginning life.)
4. understand (The others express uncertainty.)
5. perish (The others relate to eternal good.)
6. serpent (The others relate to weather.)
7. pray (The others are negative.)
8. begotten (The others relate to the story of Moses.)
9. Nicodemus (The others relate to Israel in the Old Testament.)
10. miracles (The others are negative.)

G. For God so loved the world, that he gave his only begotten Son, that whosoever believeth in him should not perish, but have everlasting life.

LESSON 5

Jesus and the Woman at the Well

Oral Reading

Encourage the children to read smoothly, with meaningful phrases.

Discussion

*Why did Jesus leave Judea?

[The Pharisees heard that Jesus was baptizing. They might have wondered if He was the Christ, but they had already started to dislike Him because He drove the buyers and sellers out of the temple. Perhaps Jesus left Judea so that the worst violence would not erupt before its time.]

Why was Jesus in Samaria?

[Samaria lay between Judea and Galilee.]

Why was Jesus alone at the well?

[The disciples had gone into the city to buy some food.]

Why did the woman come to the well?

[She came to draw water.]

What did Jesus want the woman to give Him?

[He asked her for a drink of water.]

What did He want to give to her?

[Jesus wanted to give her living water, or salvation.]

What things amazed the woman?

[She was amazed that a Jew would speak to her. She was amazed that He offered her water when He had no vessel with which to draw. And she was amazed that He knew so much about her life.]

*How did the woman know that the Messiah was coming?

[The Samaritans were partly Israelite and knew something of the Scriptures.]

*What had Jesus had to eat that the disciples did not know of?

[Jesus had satisfaction from helping a needy soul.]

What fields were ready to harvest?

[The people who needed to be saved were the harvest Jesus was talking of.]

ANSWER KEY

A.
1. land
2. tired
3. knew
4. hated
5. business
6. man
7. astonishment
8. adore
9. redemption
10. gathering

B.
1. learner, follower
2. Lord, Saviour, Christ, Messiah
3. riding, walking, running
4. request, question
5. lady, mother, wife

6. animals, cows, herds
7. hour, day, months
8. town, village

C. *Across*
1. Galilee
5. Judea
6. Philip
7. Nicodemus
9. Cana
10. Nathanael
12. Sychar
13. Bethsaida

Down
2. Elijah
3. Capernaum
4. Jerusalem
6. Peter
7. Nazareth
8. Cephas
11. Lamb

D.
1. e   5. b
2. d   6. c
3. a   7. f
4. g   8. h

E.
1. Galilee
   Samaria
   Jacob's
   Sychar
2. Samaria

saw
drink
Jews
3. me
   God
   living
   thirst / die
4. thirst
   husband

F.
1. (Any three)
   Jesus, a *Jew, asked her*, a Samaritan for a drink.
   Jesus offered her water, but *He had nothing with which to draw.*
   Jesus spoke of water that would cause one to *never thirst.*
   Jesus *knew about her past* life.
2. a. Jesus was *talking to a Samaritan* woman.
   b. Jesus spoke of *something to eat that they did not know of.*

Gradebook: 65 points
Count two points for each sentence answer—one for answer content, and one for sentence structure and form.

LESSON 6
Jesus Performs Miracles of Healing

Oral Reading
Consider the meaning and feelings in the story. Try to bring out expression with tone of voice. Have the children practice some of these sentences.

In the sentence, *"Sir, come down before my child dies,"* a sense of urgency can be expressed by emphasizing and prolonging the words *down* and *dies.*

Express gladness in the servants' report, *"Your son lives,"* by raising the voice for the word *lives.*

Convey hopelessness in the man's explanation of why he could not get into the pool to be healed by reading slowly and emphasizing *another* and *ahead*.

Discussion

Refer to the map on the inside front cover of the workbook and trace Jesus' travels from Samaria to Galilee, Cana, and Jerusalem.

Did the nobleman need a sign to believe that Jesus had healed his son?

[No, he simply went by faith in Jesus' word.]

Did the sick man at the pool need a sign before he got up and walked?

[No, he simply did what Jesus told him.]

What sign did the Jews have to help them believe in Jesus?

[They could see the man who had been sick thirty-eight years, suddenly well enough to carry his bed.]

What was it that made them criticize Jesus instead?

[They did not think it was right for a man to carry his bed on the Sabbath Day.]

*How could the man carry his bed by himself?

[Most beds in those days were simply thin mats that could be rolled up and carried.]

*Had Jesus broken the Sabbath?

[Jesus did not break God's commandment, "Remember the Sabbath Day to keep it holy." The Jews had added many details to the Law that were not given by God.]

Workbook Notes

Do number 1 of part E in class to help the pupils better understand what a summary is. Decide with them which summary is better. Point out the details in summary *a* that are not main thoughts, and also mention important points that are missing. Then assign number 2 for them to do on their own.

Many pupils are actually better at summarizing than they realize. If they find it hard to discern between items that are main thoughts and those that are not, suggest that they first write from memory a list of the things that happened. Most likely, they will automatically list the main points and leave out the secondary details.

ANSWER KEY

A.
1. nobleman
2. anxious
3. inquired
4. porch
5. troubled
6. condition
7. immediately
8. lest
9. persecuted
10. equal

B.
1. rec *ei* ved
2. f *ea* st
3. h *e*

4. h *ea* l

5. s *ee*

6. bel *ie* ved

7. f *e* ver

8. sh *ee* p

9. p *eo* ple

10. dis *ea* se

11. imm *e* diately

12. pers *e* cuted

13. *e* qual

14. J *e* sus

C.

1. S   6. M

2. S   7. M

3. M   8. S

4. S   9. M

5. M   10. M

D. (Items with answers should be underlined.)

1. (They had gone to the feast at Jerusalem and had seen the things Jesus did there.)

2. (Capernaum)

3.

4. (He was about to die.)

5.

6. (When Jesus said, "Your son lives." / At one o'clock in the afternoon)

7.

8.

9.

10. (By the sheep market)

11. (One)

12.

13.

14.

15. (Thirty-eight years)

16. (Jesus had gone away, and there were many people there.)

17. (He had healed the man on the Sabbath Day.)

18. (In the temple)

E.

1. b

2. (Sentences to be crossed out) a, c, e, g

Every time an angel troubled the waters of the pool, someone could be healed in the waters. A man who had been sick thirty-eight years lay near the pool. Jesus asked if he wanted to be made well. He wanted to be healed, but someone always got into the water ahead of him. So Jesus told the man to get up and walk. He was healed immediately, and he took up his bed and walked.

LESSON 7
Jesus Feeds the Five Thousand

Oral Reading

There are several questions in this story. Practice reading them with effective voice inflection.

"Where shall we buy bread so that these may have something to eat?"

Did Philip have *faith* that Jesus could take *care* of the people?

"But what are *they* among so many?"

"Master, when did *You* come here?"

"What *sign* do You show us then, so that we *might* see and believe? What do *You* work?"

"Will you *also* go away?"

"Lord, to *whom* shall we go?"

Quiz

Check comprehension and memory by giving this quiz orally and having the students write one of the choices given in each question.

1. Did this story take place just before or just after the Feast of the Passover?   (before)
2. Did Jesus teach the people in a mountain or on a seashore?   (in a mountain)
3. Did Jesus ask Philip where to get bread or meat?   (bread)
4. Did Peter or Andrew tell Jesus about the boy with the loaves and fish?   (Andrew)
5. Did the lad have more pieces of fish or of bread?   (bread)
6. Was it Andrew or Philip who was Simon Peter's brother?   (Andrew)
7. Did the people sit on grass or on rocks?   (grass)
8. Did Jesus break the food before or after He gave thanks?   (after)
9. Were there twelve baskets of food before or after the people ate? (after)
10. Were the people going to ask Jesus or force Him to be their king? (force)
11. Did the disciples go out on the sea in the morning or the evening? (evening)
12. Were the disciples glad or afraid when they saw Jesus walking on the sea?   (afraid)
13. Did the other people cross the sea the same day or the next day? (the next day)
14. Did they find Jesus at Capernaum or Jerusalem?   (Capernaum)
15. Did the people look for Jesus because of the miracles or because of the food?   (food)
16. Is the work of God to believe in Jesus or to heal people?   (believe in Jesus)
17. Did Jesus tell the people many things about Himself or about His disciples?   (about Himself)
18. Did more people or less people follow Him after He said these things? (less)
19. Did Peter say Jesus had the words of life or the bread of life? (words)
20. Did Jesus call Peter or Judas a devil?   (Judas)

Discussion

Help the class to make an oral summary of the story about the feeding of the five thousand. Try to identify the main points and jot them on the chalkboard, then have one student or several give the summary.

Here is a possible list of main points.

Multitudes following Jesus
Question about food
Five loaves and two fish
Five thousand men
Gave thanks and broke food
Twelve baskets full

Extra Activity

What were some of the many things Jesus told the people about Himself? Let someone report from John 6:51–57.

ANSWER KEY

A.
1. e
2. h
3. a
4. f
5. g
6. j
7. i
8. b
9. d
10. c

17. where
18. where
19. when
20. where

B.
1. when
2. where
3. where
4. where
5. when
6. when
7. when / where
8. when
9. where
10. where
11. where
12. where
13. where
14. where
15. where
16. when

C.
1. a
2. b
3. d
4. c
5. e
6. f

D.

2	5	12	15
4	8	11	13
1	6	10	14
3	7	9	16

E. (Probable numbers circled)
1, 3, 4, 5, 6, 8, 9, 11

F.
1. c
2. a
3. b
4. a
5. c

LESSON 8
The Pharisees Seek Jesus' Life

Oral Reading
Write these sentences on the chalkboard and let the children practice them with expression appropriate to the meaning.

Then He also went to the feast, but He went secretly.

They were very careful, however, to whom they told their opinions because they were afraid of the Jewish leaders.

"How does this Man know letters without ever having learned?"

"Do the rulers know for sure that this is the very Christ?"

"No man ever spoke like this Man."

Discussion
Why did Jesus stay away from Judea?

[The Jews in Judea wanted to kill Him, and it was not yet time for Him to die.]

Why did Jesus' brothers say He should go to Judea?

[They thought that if He really was the Christ, He should not hesitate to openly display His works.]

What were some of the opinions about Jesus?

[He is a good Man. He deceives the people. He is the prophet that is to come into the world. He is the Christ.]

*Had any of the rulers or any of the Pharisees believed on Jesus?

[Nicodemus may have been near believing. He spoke in favor of justice for Jesus.]

*Why did the Pharisees ask Nicodemus if he was from Galilee?

[He seemed to be supporting Jesus, and Jesus was from Galilee. They did not really suppose that Nicodemus came from Galilee, but they were mocking him because they did not think Galilee was a place where prophets and leaders came from.]

Extra Activity
Have someone report on the Feast of Tabernacles from Leviticus 23:33–36, 39–43. Information may also be found in a Bible dictionary or other reference books.

ANSWER KEY

A.
1. c
2. g
3. a
4. f
5. b
6. h
7. e
8. d

B. (Possible answers)
1. Conversation; talk about something
2. To think something will happen
3. A man in authority

4. Conclusion; idea
5. Sure evidence

C.
1. a	7. b
2. b	8. a
3. b	9. b
4. a	10. b
5. a	11. a
6. b	12. b

D.
1. His brothers
2. the world
3. Jesus
4. the Jews

5. God
6. Moses
7. the Pharisees and chief priests
8. David
9. the officers
10. Nicodemus

E.
1. yes
2. yes

F.
1. a, b	4. a, b
2. b, c	5. b, c
3. a, c	6. a, c

LESSON 9
Guilty Accusers

Oral Reading

Try to convey a cruel tone in these words:

"Now Moses in the Law commanded us that such should be stoned. But what do You say?"

A shamed tone:

"They were just as guilty of sin as she."

A compassionate tone:

"Neither do I condemn you. Go, and sin no more."

An incredulous tone:

"You are not yet fifty years old, and have You seen Abraham?"

Discussion

Why did the scribes and Pharisees report the woman's sin to Jesus?

[They wanted to catch Jesus in something they could find fault with.]

*What would have been wrong with Jesus saying that they should stone the woman?

[It could have gotten Jesus into trouble with the Roman government, because the Roman law did not allow the Jews to kill people.]

*What would have been wrong with Jesus saying that the woman should not be stoned?

[The Jews could have accused Him of breaking Moses' Law, and they probably would have used that to turn the people against Him.]

*When is it right to report the bad things someone has done?

[It is right if it helps the person who does wrong to change his ways. It is not right if we do it out of meanness, wanting to get others into trouble. Neither is it right if we do it to make ourselves look good by comparison.]

*What do you think Jesus was writing on the ground?
  [Perhaps He wrote something that made the men think of their own sins,
  such as other parts of the Law which they had broken.]
Was Jesus thinking of Abraham as dead?
  [No, He knew Abraham was living with God after his life on earth.]

ANSWER KEY

A.
1. S
2. A
3. S
4. S
5. S
6. A
7. A
8. A
9. A
10. S
11. S
12. S
13. A
14. A
15. S

B.
1. adultery
2. tempt
3. consciences
4. hypocrites
5. Abraham

C.
1.
2. but had broken
3. and blame Him
4. and pretenders
5. by Himself
6. and seek
7. and keep on
8. and words
9. and untruth
10. and were sure
11. and told them
12. and full of nonsense
13. nearly

D.
1. b, c
2. a, c
3. c, e, f
4. b, d

E.
1. possibly
2. themselves
3. hardly
4. certain
5. there
6. exactly
7. free
8. big
9. Jesus
10. now

F. (Possible summary)

The scribes and Pharisees brought a woman who had committed adultery and asked Jesus what should be done to her. Jesus did not answer but stooped and wrote on the ground. When they kept asking, He said the one without any sin should throw the first stone. The scribes and Pharisees all left because they had sin in their lives. Jesus said to the woman, "Neither do I condemn you. Go, and sin no more."

LESSON 10
Sight and Salvation for a Blind Man

Oral Reading

How is the volume in oral reading? If the students need help to read more loudly, stand across the room from them and have them increase volume until you can hear them well. You might step out of sight to stimulate the natural impulse to raise the voice for talking to someone in another room.

Discussion

What did the disciples think was the reason for the man's blindness?

[They thought it was punishment for sin.]

What was truly the reason that he was blind?

[He was blind so that Jesus could show God's power by healing him.]

*How can hardships today display God's power?

[God still helps His people through their problems in life. When other people see how God helps them, it brings honor to His Name.]

*Was it the clay that healed the man's eyes? Why did Jesus make it?

[No, it was the power of Jesus that healed the man's eyes. Jesus did not need the clay to heal the man, but He chose to do it that way.]

What were the conflicting opinions about Jesus, and why?

[This Man is not of God, because He did this on the Sabbath Day. This Man is of God, because no one else ever gave sight to a man born blind.]

*Why did the Pharisees keep asking the man how he was healed?

[They probably wanted a confession that would give them an excuse to cast him out of the synagogue so that others would fear.]

What did the man say that made the Pharisees think he was trying to teach them?

[He explained that God does not hear sinners, but God heard Jesus and gave Him power to do miracles.]

ANSWER KEY

A.
1. d	6. g
2. c	7. j
3. f	8. e
4. i	9. b
5. a	10. h

B.
1. 3	7. 2	13. 3
2. 1	8. 3	14. 3
3. 2	9. 2	15. 3
4. 2	10. 1	16. 1
5. 3	11. 3	17. 3
6. 3	12. 2	18. 2

C. (Sentences to be marked with *X*)

2, 3, 4, 5, 7, 8, 10

D.
1. the disciples
2. Jesus
3. the blind man
4. neighbors and others who had seen him before, (or) Pharisees
5. neighbors and others who had seen him before
6. Pharisees
7. the man who had been blind

8. Pharisees
9. the man's parents
10. Pharisees
11. the man who had been blind
12. Jesus

E.   1. The man was born blind so that *the works of God might be shown* in him.
       2. The Pharisees were displeased because Jesus *healed* the man *on the Sabbath Day.*

3. The Pharisees were displeased because the *man said Jesus was of God.*

F.   3   1
       4   2
       5   6

Gradebook: 58 points, counting two points for each sentence answer in part E, and two points for part F

LESSON 11
The Good Shepherd

Oral Reading

Remind the students to read loudly enough to be clearly heard. Require rereading if you are not satisfied with the volume.

Discussion

In comparing a shepherd and his sheep to God and His people, who does the shepherd represent?

[The shepherd is Jesus.]

Who are the sheep?

[The sheep are God's people.]

Who are the "other sheep" of a different fold?

[Other sheep are the people who turn to God from groups other than the Jews.]

*What is the sheepfold?

[The fold could be the Christian church or it could be heaven.]

*Who are the strangers, thieves, and robbers?

[They are people who teach false things and try to get Christians to turn away from God.]

*Who are hirelings?

[Hirelings are leaders in churches who want the position for their own honor or gain.]

What were the Jews to do to a man who claimed to be God?

[They were to stone him.]

Why should the Jews have known that Jesus is God and not a man pretending to be God?

[They should have believed Jesus because He did the works of God.]

ANSWER KEY

A. 1. perish 7. sheepfold
2. eternal 8. shepherd
3. doubt 9. pluck
4. porter 10. kill
5. thieves 11. hirelings
6. recognize 12. miracles

B. 1. understand
2. sheepfold
3. doorkeeper
4. sometimes / someone
5. wintertime
6. everything

C. 1. porter 5. dedication
2. abundantly 6. blasphemy
3. hireling 7. angered
4. Jews 8. escaped

D. *Across*
4. sheepfold 16. who
5. not 17. pasture
8. wall 18. wolf
9. porter 20. Door
12. recognize 21. robbers
14. voice

Down
1. before 10. rejoice
2. power 11. follow
3. kill 13. guard
6. open 15. pen
7. name 19. go

E. 1. wintertime
2. in the temple in Solomon's porch
3. no
4. Jesus had done many miracles.
5. Everything John had said about Jesus was true.

F. (Words may vary.)
1. Jesus and the Woman at the Well, sit / ride, cars
2. Jesus Feeds the Five Thousand, stands
3. John the Baptist Reveals Jesus, church
4. The Beginning of Jesus' Ministry, faucet / spigot
5. Guilty Accusers, prison / jail
6. Jesus Performs Miracles of Healing, one

LESSON 12
A Death for the Glory of God

Oral Reading

Pay attention to clear pronunciation of all syllables, especially in the multisyllable words. You may want to list some of these words on the chalkboard for practice.

glorified disciples Lazarus Bethany
nevertheless resurrection secretly hastily

Discussion

What did Mary and Martha want of Jesus when they sent for Him?
[They wanted Him to heal their brother.]

Did Jesus come right away?   [No.]

When Jesus did come, did they get what they wanted?   [Yes.]

   Sometimes when we pray, it might seem that God does not answer. Sometimes His answer is, "Wait a while," and things may seem to get worse for a time. In the case of Lazarus, God received more glory by raising him from the dead than by healing him of sickness. God's way is always best.

*Why was Jesus glad Lazarus had died?

   [He knew the resurrection of Lazarus would help His disciples to believe in Him.]

What did Thomas think would happen if they went to Judea?

   [He thought they would all be stoned.]

*What did the people not understand about Jesus' work or ways?

   [They thought His power was limited by death, and there was no hope for Lazarus any more. Note: It was a common belief that after three days, the spirit departed from the body never to return.]

ANSWER KEY

A. 1. glorify
   2. glory
   3. glorified
   4. lately
   5. latest
   6. late
   7. rise
   8. resurrection
   9. risen
   10. clothes
   11. grave
   12. grave clothes

B. 1. lie
   2. lie
   3. lay
   4. lay
   5. lie

C. 1. lay
   2. lay
   3. laid
   4. laid
   5. lay

D. 1. Nazareth
   2. Lazarus
   3. Bethany
   4. Bethlehem
   5. Nicodemus
   6. Capernaum
   7. Zebedee
   8. Galilee
   9. Bethsaida
   10. Samaria

E. 1. b   4. a
   2. b   5. b
   3. a   6. a

F. 1. yes
   2. yes
   3. yes
   4. yes
   5. no
      She said he would rise in the resurrection at the last day. (or) She protested when Jesus asked to have the stone rolled away.

G. 1. The people had to *help Lazarus get loose from the grave clothes* in which he was wrapped.

2. It was a greater miracle to raise a dead man than to heal a sick man. *It helped more people to believe* on Jesus.

LESSON 13
"Blessed Is the King of Israel!"

Oral Reading

Demonstrate clear enunciation by reading a sentence with mumbled, slurred syllables and then reading the same sentence with every syllable clearly pronounced. Have the students read small portions, concentrating on reading every syllable clearly.

Discussion

What did the chief priests and Pharisees think the Romans would do if everybody believed on Jesus?

[The Romans would take away their place and nation.]

*What was the place and nation of the Pharisees?

[Their nation was the Jewish people. The Romans ruled over the Jews, but they allowed the religious leaders to have a place of authority among the Jews. If everybody followed Jesus instead of the Pharisees, the Romans might remove the Pharisees from any authority.]

*How did Caiaphas think it would save the nation if one man died?

[If Jesus died, everything could go on as before, and their nation would not be destroyed.]

In what other way was it true that one Man would die to save the nation?

[Jesus would die as an atonement for sin to save all people from hell.]

What did the Pharisees tell the people to do when they knew where Jesus was?

[The people were to tell the Pharisees so that they could arrest Jesus.]

What did the people do when they heard that Jesus was coming?

[They went out with palm branches and cried, "Hosanna! Blessed is the King of Israel!"]

Were the Pharisees getting the support that they expected as leaders?

[No.]

ANSWER KEY

A.				**B.**			
1. b		6. a		1. miracle		6. spikenard
2. b		7. b		2. foretell		7. expensive
3. a		8. a		3. counseled		8. odor
4. b		9. a		4. purify		9. burial
5. b		10. a		5. arrest		10. fulfill

C. 1. Romans
2. Ephraim
3. Martha
4. feet
5. himself
6. Lazarus
7. donkey
8. Zechariah

3. Judas was a thief, and *he wanted the money.*
4. Lazarus' life was *a reminder of Jesus' power.*
5. Jesus rode on a donkey *to fulfill what the prophet said* about Him in the Scriptures.

D. 1. *God gave him the wisdom* to say it.
2. They went to Jerusalem *to purify themselves.*

E. 1. before   4. middle
2. again   5. wrong
3. not   6. too much

LESSON 14
Death Leads to Life

Oral Reading

Remind the students to pronounce every syllable clearly.

Discussion

In what were the Pharisees not succeeding?

[They were not succeeding in arresting Jesus.]

*What was their real concern in seeing the world go after Jesus?

[They were angry about losing their influence and were afraid of losing their position.]

What was Jesus' reply when Philip and Andrew told Him some men wanted to see Him?

["The hour has come that the Son of Man should be glorified."]

*What did that answer have to do with their request?

[The time was near that Jesus would die. In this He would be made known to all men.]

What must die before a plant can grow?

[The seed must die.]

What must die before spiritual life can grow?

[A man must die to his self-will.]

*In what way did Jesus die to self?

[He did not give in to the desire to save Himself from death.]

How could the Christ live forever if Jesus was to die?

[Jesus would rise again and live forever.]

Why did many people not believe in Jesus?

[They did not want to believe. They did not want to give up their own ways.]

ANSWER KEY

A.
1. d 6. e
2. g 7. c
3. a 8. f
4. h 9. b
5. j 10. i

B.
1. comprehend
2. reveals
3. scourge
4. bridegroom
5. tarried
6. parcel
7. infirmity
8. sufficient
9. doctrine
10. consulted

C. (Answers may vary.)
1. followed Jesus.
2. sprout and make a new plant.
3. spiritual life.
4. "Father, glorify Your Name."
5. Christ lives forever.
6. they did not want to believe.
7. they were afraid of the Pharisees.

D.
1. a 4. a
2. b 5. b
3. a

E.
1. E 8. D
2. B 9. B
3. B 10. D
4. D 11. B
5. D 12. E
6. B
7. E

Gradebook: 44 points

LESSON 15
The Last Supper

Oral Reading

Discuss the feelings and expression of Peter's objection to having Jesus wash his feet. Encourage the children to read the conversation in a realistic way.

Discussion

*Why is this Passover supper called the Last Supper?

[It was the last meal Jesus ate before His crucifixion.]

What was unusual about a Lord and Master washing His servants' feet?

[Washing feet was a very lowly service, performed by servants for their masters.]

Why did Jesus give a sop to Judas?

[He gave the sop as an indication of who would be the traitor. The sop was also an expression of Jesus' love for Judas.]

Did the disciples understand that Judas would be the traitor?

[No.]

ANSWER KEY

A. 1. enemies
2. example
3. disciples
4. basin
5. defiled
6. necessary
7. cleansed (or) washed
8. troubled
9. verily
10. bosom
11. perhaps
12. supper / feast
13. sop
14. immediately

B. 1. Servant
2. Master
3. Example
4. Saviour
5. King of kings
6. Word

C. 1. c   6. b
2. c   7. c
3. a   8. a
4. a   9. b
5. b   10. a

D. 1. *Satan* put into Judas's heart to betray Jesus.
2. Jesus was *washing* His disciples' *feet*.
3. Peter *wanted to belong to Jesus* as much as he could.
4. They thought Judas was going to *buy something* for the feast or *give something* to the poor.
5. Jesus taught His disciples to *love one another*.

LESSON 16
Jesus Teaches the Troubled Disciples

Quiz

Give these statements orally to test silent reading comprehension. Have the children write *true* or *false* on a numbered paper.

(false)   1. Jesus told His disciples He would go where they could never follow.

(true)   2. Peter said he would die for Jesus' sake.

(false)   3. Jesus said Peter would deny Him three times before the sun went down.

(false)   4. The disciples were troubled because they heard the cock crow.

(true)   5. Jesus told of many mansions in His Father's house.

(false)   6. The disciples would go with Jesus to help Him prepare their place.

(true)   7. Jesus is the Way, the Truth, and the Life.

(true)   8. No man comes to God except by Jesus.

(true)   9. Those who believe on Jesus will do the works that He does, and even greater works.

(true)	10. God will do what the believers ask in Jesus' Name.
(true)	11. The Comforter whom Jesus promised to send would be the Holy Spirit.
(false)	12. The Holy Spirit would stay with the disciples for only a short time.
(false)	13. The Holy Spirit would teach things that were different from what Jesus said.
(false)	14. Jesus used the example of an olive tree to illustrate a truth.
(true)	15. Dead branches are gathered and burned.
(true)	16. Fruitful branches are trimmed to make them bear more fruit.
(true)	17. In the illustration, Jesus' followers are the branches.
(false)	18. In the illustration, God is the soil in which the plant grows.
(false)	19. The Holy Spirit is the caretaker of the vine.
(false)	20. The good works of the disciples are the leaves on the branches.

Oral Reading

The disciples were troubled by the things Jesus was saying to them. Tell the children to think of how the disciples felt, and read the discussion in a tone that fits the feeling.

Workbook Note

In part D, point out key words that will help the pupils to make the correct choices. Here are a few examples: number 1—*never deceive*; number 2—*entrance*; and number 3—*helps man to see.*

ANSWER KEY

A.
1. denied
2. mansions
3. presence
4. providence
5. dwells
6. compress
7. ability
8. illustrate
9. prune
10. century

B.
1. kine
2. ox
3. roebuck
4. turtle ⎫ interchangeable
5. snail ⎭
6. ant
7. ostrich
8. cock

9. swine
10. bat
11. donkey
12. serpent
13. ram
14. wolf
15. sheep
16. bear
17. hare
18. spider
19. owl
20. lion

C.
1. a. "Lord, where are You going?"
   b. "Lord, why can I not follow You now?"
2. "Lord, we do not know where You are going, and how can we know the way?"
3. "Lord, show us the Father, and that will satisfy us."
4. Jesus promised that He would *send them the Holy Spirit.*

5. God would *do whatever the disciples asked* in Jesus' Name.
6. The Holy Ghost would *teach them* all things and *bring to memory* what Jesus had said.

D.
1. I am the Truth.
2. I am the Door of the sheep.
3. I am the Light of the world.

4. I am the Vine.
5. I am the Good Shepherd.
6. I am the Resurrection.
7. I am the Life.
8. I am the Way.
9. I am the Bread of Life.

E.
1. God
2. Christians
3. Jesus
4. Good works

LESSON 17
Jesus Prepares the Disciples

Oral Reading

Pay attention again to the conversation in the story and encourage realistic expression.

Discussion

*For what was Jesus preparing His disciples?

[He was preparing them to face hard things—the hatred of the world, persecution by the Jews, and sorrow at His death.]

How did He prepare the disciples?

[He told them the truth about what they would face.]

Sometimes the truth hurts, but it is much kinder to be honest about hard things than to deceive people by saying things we think they would like to hear.

What was the advantage of being friends instead of servants of Jesus?

[Jesus shared His purpose more completely and clearly with His friends. Some of the things He shared were hard to understand and caused them sorrow, but it was worth it to be close friends with Jesus.]

What would be a comfort to the disciples in the hard things they would face?

[The Holy Ghost would be with them and comfort them.]

*What was the meaning of "A little while, and you shall not see Me, and again a little while, and you shall see Me"?

[It would not be long until Jesus died and was separated from His disciples. But then it would not be long until He rose and could be with His disciples again.]

ANSWER KEY

A.
1. g	9. k
2. c	10. p
3. a	11. o
4. h	12. m
5. f	13. i
6. b	14. j
7. d	15. n
8. e	16. l

B. Comforter, Holy Ghost, Spirit of Truth

C. (The numbers to the left side of the design tell which questions pertain to each row. Italicized numbers are questions that would mar the pattern.)

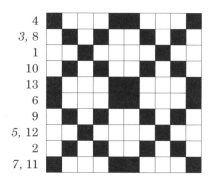

D.
1. A friend *knows* things that a servant does not.
2. They were *not able to bear* everything at that time.
3. The *Spirit of Truth* would teach them all things.

E.
1. c	5. b
2. a	6. a
3. a	7. c
4. c	

LESSON 18
Jesus Betrayed and Arrested

Oral Reading

Encourage expression that conveys the agitation of Peter with his sword, the calmness of Jesus yielding Himself, and the frenzy of Peter's denial.

Discussion

Where was Judas when Jesus and the rest of the disciples went to the garden?
[Judas was settling his agreement with the chief priests and Pharisees, and preparing the band of men for the arrest.]

How did he know where Jesus was?
[Jesus often went to this garden.]

*What made the officers fall backward when Jesus spoke?
[A supernatural power made them fall, which displayed again that Jesus is the Son of God.]

Could Jesus have gotten away if He wanted to?   [Yes]

*Why did He not escape?
[He knew that the time had come that He should die to save sinners, and He was willing to bear that suffering.]

*What did Jesus mean when He said, "The cup which My Father has given Me, shall I not drink it?"

[A "cup to drink" was an expression that meant one's condition of life. God had planned this experience for Jesus, and He was not going to refuse or fight against it.]

*What do you think the high priest wanted Jesus to say when he asked Him about His disciples and teaching?

[He probably wanted Jesus to plainly say that He is the Son of God. Then he would accuse Jesus of blasphemy, which would be a lawful reason to have Him put to death.]

ANSWER KEY

A.

1. 5	5. 5	9. 5	13. 5
3	2	4	1
4	1	2	3
1	3	3	4
2	4	1	2

2. 3	6. 1	10. 5	14. 5
1	3	2	3
4	2	3	2
2	5	4	4
5	4	1	1

3. 4	7. 2	11. 4	15. 3
1	3	1	4
3	5	2	1
5	1	3	2
2	4	5	5

4. 3	8. 5	12. 1	16. 4
2	1	5	5
4	3	4	3
5	4	3	1
1	2	2	2

B.
1. sheath
2. disciple
3. sword
4. Kidron
5. coals
6. weapons
7. immediately
8. relative

C.
1. when
2. where
3. why
4. when
5. where
6. why
7. when
8. where
9. where
10. where
11. when
12. where
13. why
14. when
15. when
16. where

D.
1. a band of men and officers
2. Peter
3. Annas
4. a girl / doorkeeper
5. the high priest / Caiaphas
6. one of the officers

E.
1. a   3. a   5. c
2. c   4. b   6. a

LESSON 19
Jesus Before Pilate

Oral Reading
Do not compromise correct reading while practicing expressive reading. If necessary, remind the class to read exactly what is printed and to pronounce each syllable clearly.

Discussion
*Why would the Jews be in trouble if they killed Jesus?
[The Romans ruled the Jews and did not allow them to kill a man, even though he was guilty according to their law.]
*How would going into the Judgment Hall make the Jews unclean?
[The Judgment Hall was a place of the Gentiles. The Jews considered it such an unholy place that if they entered, they would not be holy enough to partake of the Passover Feast.]
Why was Pilate uneasy about condemning Jesus?
[The Jews' accusation was that Jesus made Himself the Son of God. If indeed He was the Son of God, Pilate was afraid of God's judgment.]
Whose power would Pilate fear if he let Jesus go?
[Caesar's. He might be in trouble with the king if he released someone else who claimed to be the king.]

Extra Activity
Have the children write sentences for some of the unused words in part B.

ANSWER KEY

A.
1. purple
2. pretending
3. prisoners
4. priests
5. permission
6. power
7. Passover
8. particular
10. distance
11. entire
12. tidy

B.
1. shaggy
2. recent
3. dismay
4. approaching
5. conceal
6. famous
7. mingle
8. collide
9. prevent

C.
1. Pilate
2. Jews
3. Pilate
4. Pilate
5. Jesus
6. Jesus
7. Pilate
8. Pilate
9. Jews
10. Pilate
11. Jews
12. Pilate
13. Jesus
14. Jesus
15. Jews

D.
1. The Jews had to have *permission* from the Roman government to kill anyone.
2. Going into the Hall of Judgment would *defile* them for eating the Passover.

3. They said He ought to die because He *made Himself the Son of God.*
4. They put a *crown of thorns* on His head, *made fun of* Him, and *hit* Him.
5. They pretended to be Caesar's friends because they wanted *to have Jesus killed.*

E. 1. b
2. c
3. a

Gradebook: 48 points, counting two for each sentence answer in part D

LESSON 20
Jesus Gives His Life

Oral Reading
This story has several exclamation points. Call attention to them and the expression they indicate.

Discussion
Where was Jesus crucified?

[At "the place of a skull"]

*Why was it called the place of a skull?

[It may have been that the hill resembled a skull in appearance. Or the name may have been applied as a symbol of death because of the executions that took place there.]

In what three languages was the title on Jesus' cross written?

[Hebrew, Greek, and Latin]

*Why were those languages used?

[Hebrew was the language of the Jews and the Old Testament Scriptures. Greek was the formal language of the educated Romans. Latin was the everyday language spoken by the Romans. Everyone who went by would be able to understand what was written.]

Who was the disciple that cared for Jesus' mother after this?

[The beloved disciple, John]

Extra Activity
Let the students find in the Old Testament the prophecies fulfilled in this story. Use a concordance and look up *vesture, thirst, broken,* and *pierced.* [Psalm 22:18; Psalm 69:21; Psalm 34:20; Zechariah 12:10].

It may be interesting to compare the wording of the Old Testament prophecies with the New Testament quotes.

ANSWER KEY

A. *Across*

1. spear
6. languages
8. cross
10. vinegar
11. vesture
13. Caesar
15. perfumes
16. Hebrew
18. guilty
21. title
22. hyssop
23. near
24. bone
25. sepulcher

Down

1. son
2. sponge
3. two
4. woven
5. Magdalene
6. legs
7. skull
8. crucifixion
9. spices
11. vessel
12. seams
13. Cleophas
14. Latin
17. Pilate
19. death
20. cast

B.

1. d	10. m	
2. e	11. j	
3. b	12. n	
4. a	13. k	
5. c	14. l	
6. i	15. p	
7. f	16. q	
8. g	17. o	
9. h	18. r	

C.

3	13	17
5	15	19
7	11	22
6	14	20
1	12	21
8	9	23
2	16	24
4	10	18

D. (Order interchangeable)

1. The soldiers divided *Jesus' clothes* and cast lots for His coat.
2. Jesus was given *vinegar to drink*.
3. Jesus' *bones were not broken*.
4. A soldier *pierced* His side with a spear.

E.

1. T	7. B	
2. P	8. B	
3. T	9. P	
4. P	10. T	
5. P	11. B	
6. T	12. B	

LESSON 21
Joy After Sorrow

Oral Reading

Reflect the excitement of the empty tomb and the realization of the resurrection.

Discussion

*What day came between the last story and this one?

[The Sabbath Day. Jesus was buried hurriedly before the Sabbath began, and Mary waited until after the Sabbath to go to the tomb.]

Who was the other disciple with Peter?

[The beloved disciple, John]

Who was the first person to realize that Jesus was risen?

[Mary Magdalene]

When did she realize this?

[She thought someone had removed His body until Jesus said her name.]

*Do you think it was something different to have the doors closed when the disciples gathered together?

[Gathering behind closed doors probably means they had the doors locked or barred so that no one could enter.]

*How did Jesus get in?

[In His resurrected body, Jesus was not limited to normal human abilities. He could instantly be somewhere regardless of the obstructions between.]

Workbook Note

Give special help for part E. Tell the children to pretend they are Mary Magdalene and have them formulate some sentences orally to illustrate.

ANSWER KEY

A.
1. resurrection (The others relate to death.)
2. evening (The others are verbs.)
3. believing (The others are disbelieving.)
4. ascended (The others relate to being together.)
5. stone (The others are fabric.)
6. Thomas (The others are deity.)
7. weeping (The others are pleasant things.)
8. Sabbath (The others are disciples.)
9. napkin (The others are parts of the body.)
10. gathered (The others are people.)

B.
1. c
2. e
3. f
4. a
5. d
6. b
7. h
8. j
9. i
10. l
11. g
12. k

13. q	19. x
14. p	20. w
15. r	21. s
16. o	22. t
17. m	23. v
18. n	24. u

C.
1. last
2. saw
3. went
4. Mary
5. Thomas
6. Jews
7. glad

D.
1. It was still *dark* when she went to the sepulcher.
2. Both John and Mary *stooped* to look inside.
3. Jesus *showed the marks* to the disciples and especially to Thomas.

4. The grave clothes *remained in the sepulcher*, and Jesus appeared so much like an ordinary man that Mary thought He was the *caretaker*.

E. (Individual work)
(The account should be written in the first person and include these points:)
The man who spoke to her
Her offer to take Jesus' body
Jesus says her name
His message to the brethren

LESSON 22
Jesus and the Disciples at the Seashore

Oral Reading

The words spoken between Jesus on the shore and the disciples in the ship must have been called across some distance, as the disciples did not recognize Jesus. This is a good opportunity to emphasize volume in reading.

Discussion

*Why did Jesus call His disciples children?
[He loved them tenderly as His children.]
Who recognized Jesus?
[The beloved disciple, John]
*What made this disciple recognize Him?
[He probably recognized Jesus because of the miracle of the great catch of fish. A similar miracle had happened before; see Luke 5:4–10.]
*Where did Jesus get the bread and the fish on the coals?
[He may have miraculously produced that too.]
Who were the lambs and sheep that Peter was supposed to feed?
[They were the people who would believe in Jesus.]
*What would Peter feed them?
[Peter would feed them spiritually by preaching about Jesus.]

What did Jesus say about John that made the brethren think he would not die?

[Jesus said, "If I will that he tarries till I come, what is that to you?"]

*Did John tarry till Jesus came?

[No, but John did live to see the vision of Jesus' coming when he was on the Isle of Patmos. He was also the only one of the twelve disciples to die a natural death. However, Jesus' question was not a promise, but simply an illustration to teach Peter that it should not concern him what John was to do.]

ANSWER KEY

A.
1. a, b, d
2. b, c, d
3. a, c, d
4. b, c, d
5. a, b, c
6. a, b, d

7. a, c, d
8. a, b, c
9. a, c, d
10. a, b, d
11. b, c, d
12. a, b, d

13. a, b, d
14. a, c, d
15. b, c, d
16. a, c, d
17. b, c, d
18. a, b, c

B.

		4. 1	7. 3
		3	1
		4	4
		2	2
2. 2	5. 4	8. 4
4	1	2
1	2	3
3	3	1
3. 1	6. 3	9. 3
2	2	2
3	1	4
4	4	1

C.
1. Simon Peter
2. seven
3. in the night
4. children
5. the disciple whom Jesus loved / John
6. one hundred fifty-three
7. three
8. Feed My lambs. Feed My sheep.
9. John
10. no

D.
1. Peter *threw himself into the sea* and swam or waded.
2. He was talking about the way *Peter would die.*
3. There would be so many books the *world could not hold them all.*

E.
1. a, c
2. b, c, d
3. a, b, c
4. a, c, d
5. a, b, c, d
6. b, c, d
7. a, d
8. a, b, d
9. a, d
10. a, c, d

TEST

ANSWER KEY

A.
1. b		11. p
2. d		12. o
3. f		13. k
4. h		14. s
5. i		15. t
6. e		16. l
7. a		17. n
8. g		18. m
9. j		19. r
10. c		20. q

B.
1. Simon Peter
2. Judas Iscariot
3. Thomas
4. John the Baptist
5. Cephas
6. Andrew
7. Nicodemus
8. Lazarus
9. Pilate
10. Caiaphas

C.
5	6	14
2	9	12
1	10	15
3	8	11
4	7	13

D.
1. Jesus said this to *Nicodemus* when He *talked with him at night.*
2. Jesus said this to the *Samaritan woman* when He was *at a well.*
3. Jesus said this to the *woman* taken in adultery when the *scribes and Pharisees accused her* before Him.
4. Jesus said this to *Judas* when he left the *Passover supper* to betray Jesus.
5. Jesus said this to *Pilate* during His *trial.*

Gradebook: 46 test points, counting two points for each set in part C and two for each number in part D

Unit Two

The Book of Acts

UNIT 2
General Plan

The lessons in Unit 2 are based on stories from the Book of Acts.

Help make these stories live by using a map. The ideal way is to have a large wall map. Such a map, titled *Journeys of Paul Project Map*, is available from Rod and Staff Publishers. Or a map could be drawn by enlarging the one on pages 48 and 49 of the pupil's workbook. Locate the setting of the wall map on a globe.

Every time a place is mentioned in oral reading, have someone locate it on the map. Encourage the students to refer to it often as they read silently.

The unit test in the back of the pupil's workbook should be removed and filed before the workbooks are distributed.

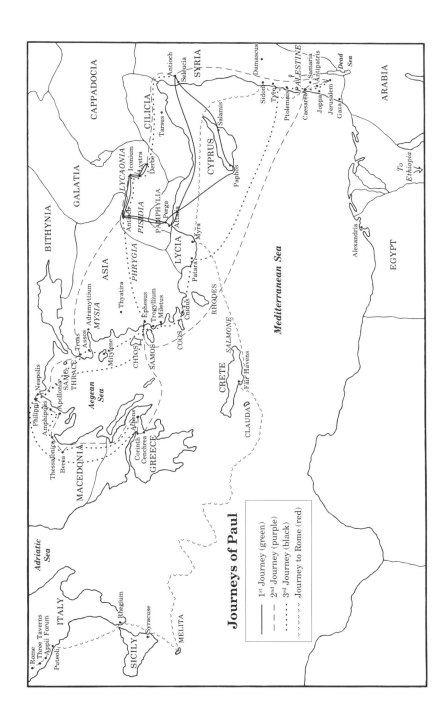

Journeys of Paul

——————	1st Journey (green)
– – – – –	2nd Journey (purple)
··········	3rd Journey (black)
∿∿∿∿∿	Journey to Rome (red)

Unit 2   Lessons

LESSON 1
Introduction to Acts
and
The Ascension of Jesus

Oral Reading

How do you pronounce *apostle*? The *t* is silent just as in *whistle* or *castle*. Pay special attention to correct pronunciation of all the names.

Discussion

Who were the apostles?

[The apostles were the twelve chosen disciples whom Jesus gave a special charge to preach and do miracles. (The word *disciples* in Unit 1 usually meant these twelve men. In this unit *disciples* refers to the broader group of believers.)]

Who were the four emperors named in the lesson?

[Augustus Caesar, Tiberius Caesar, Claudius Caesar, and Nero]

*Why were there Herods and Caesars ruling at the same time?

[The Caesars in Rome were the highest Roman rulers. The Herods in Palestine were given a position of local rule by Caesar.]

How far was it from Jerusalem to the Mount of Olives?

[The Mount of Olives was a Sabbath Day's journey from Jerusalem.]

*Why was the distance called a Sabbath Day's journey?

[The Jews had many rules about what should or should not be done on the Sabbath Day. One of them was a limit to the distance they were allowed to travel. A Sabbath Day's journey was two thousand cubits, which would be less than a mile.]

Why did Peter think someone should be ordained to take Judas's place?

[The Scriptures prophesied of Judas and said, "Let another man take his office."]

Workbook Note

If children have trouble with part C, they may have missed the title.

ANSWER KEY

A.
1. (a•grip' ə)
2. (ä•gus' tus)
3. (bär' sə•bəs)
4. (bär•thol' o•mū)
5. (klô' di•us)
6. (it' ə•lē)
7. (ma•thī' əs)
8. (nē' rō)
9. (pal' is•tīn)
10. (tī•bē' ri•us)
11. (zē•lō' tēz)

B.
1. g
2. e
3. f
4. a
5. b
6. i
7. h
8. c
9. d

C. (Any three—You may also accept *mention* and *section*, which appear in the story with suffixes.)
introduction, ascension, resurrection, supplication

D. *Disciples*   *Roman Rulers*

Simon	Augustus
Judas	Caesar
Matthias	Tiberius
Philip	Herod
Barsabas	Claudius
Bartholomew	Agrippa
Peter	Nero

E.
1. a   4. b
2. b   5. a
3. b   6. c

7. b   12. b
8. c   13. b
9. b   14. a
10. a   15. b
11. c

F.   (Possible answers)
1. There were about one hundred twenty disciples gathered in the room.
2. The apostles may have been hoping to catch another glimpse of Jesus.

LESSON 2
The Day of Pentecost

Oral Reading

Notice the clues to the tone of voice for these quotations.

In *wonder* and *amazement* they said, "Look, are not all these who speak Galileans? How can we all understand them in our own language in which we were born?"

Others *mocked* the disciples. "These men are full of new wine," they said.

They felt so *guilty* that they asked, "Men and brethren, what shall we do?"

Discussion

What did the disciples begin to do when the Holy Ghost filled them?
 [They began to speak in other languages.]
*Why was it helpful to have many different languages spoken?
 [There were people from many different nations at Jerusalem. Through this miracle, they could all understand the Gospel being preached.]
*Does the Holy Ghost cause Christians to speak in different languages today?
 [In a time of unusual need for other languages to be understood, God has wrought such miracles in our day. But He does not do this without a special purpose or for the display of the speaker. When God causes such things to happen, the words of the speaker can be understood.]
*Why was the time of day an indication that the men were not drunk?
 [It was more normal for people to be drunk at the end of the day than at the beginning.]

How many people were baptized that day?

[About three thousand believers were baptized that day.]

What did the people in the new church do day by day?

[They gathered at the temple to worship every day.]

How were meals and other needs provided for these people?

[They all shared their things. Some of them sold their property and divided the money among the needy.]

Extra Activity

Find the prophecy quoted from Joel by looking up the word *spirit* in the concordance. [Joel 2:28]

Find the prophecy quoted from Psalms by looking up the word *corruption*. [Psalm 16:10]

ANSWER KEY

A.
1. 3
2. 3
3. 3
4. 2
5. 3
6. 3
7. 4
8. 2
9. 3
10. 2
11. 3
12. 3
13. 1
14. 3
15. 4

12. Joel
13. David
14. rushing mighty wind
15. divided
16. new

B.
1. a. languages
   b. words to speak
2. sincere and religious
3. a. the news spread
   b. perplexed and confused
4. decay

C.
1. 10
2. 50
3. 40
4. 10
5. nine o'clock
6. 3,000
7. Galilee
8. many different nations
9. Jerusalem
10. Nazareth
11. Peter

D.
1. The disciples spoke the *wonderful works of God.*
2. There were people in Jerusalem from *many nations.*
3. a. "What does this mean?"
   b. "These men are full of new wine."
4. They were filled with the *Holy Ghost* who gave them words to speak.
5. Peter told them to *repent and be baptized.*
6. They *sold* the things they owned and *shared* the money.

LESSON 3
Peter and John in the Temple

Oral Reading

Encourage expression to convey excitement about the lame man's healing and the displeasure of the Jewish rulers.

Discussion

How long had the man at the temple gate been lame?

[He was lame ever since his birth, and he was more than forty years old.]

*Why was the gate of the temple a good place for the lame man to be?

[Religious people gave alms, and the temple gate was a place where he would meet many religious people.]

Peter said, "What I do have, I will give to you." What did Peter have to give?

[He had the power of Jesus to heal.]

*After the miracle, a crowd of people gathered around Peter and the healed man. Why was Peter concerned about this?

[Peter was afraid that the people would give him the credit and exalt him as a great man. He wanted to be sure they knew it was through Jesus that the man was healed.]

Why did the priests, the captain of the temple, and the Sadducees become displeased?

[They did not want the Name of Jesus to be exalted.]

What did the rulers do to keep the message about Jesus from spreading?

[They commanded Peter and John to no longer teach in the Name of Jesus.]

Were their efforts successful?

[No, the believers prayed for boldness to speak the Word of God, and then they spoke the Word with boldness.]

ANSWER KEY

A. 1. (Any five)
   Jesus Christ
   Son Jesus
   Holy One
   Just
   Prince of Life
   Stone
 2. (Any ten)

Peter	Pilate
John	Sadducees
Solomon	Annas
Israel	Caiaphas
Abraham	Alexander
Isaac	David
Jacob	Herod

3. (Any fifteen)

man	captain
people	disciples
poor	elders
men	heathen
fathers	scribes
murderer	high priest
apostles	builders
brethren	relatives
rulers	company
prophets	believers
priest(s)	

B. (Possible answers)

1. Money or gifts to help the poor
2. Refused to accept (acknowledge)
3. Good health
4. Without knowledge (training)
5. Say what will be done to hurt or punish

C.

1.	no	11.	yes
2.	no	12.	no
3.	yes	13.	no
4.	no	14.	no
5.	yes	15.	yes
6.	yes	16.	no
7.	yes	17.	yes
8.	no	18.	no
9.	yes	19.	yes
10.	yes	20.	yes

D.

1.	a	4.	c
2.	c	5.	b
3.	a	6.	a

Gradebook: 61 points

LESSON 4
Ananias and Sapphira

Oral Reading

Explain and demonstrate a lowered tone for reading subordinate sentence parts. These contain facts that make the story clearer, but oral reading is more meaningful if such parts receive less emphasis. Some practice sentences are listed here.

The apostles had named him Barnabas, *which means "son of consolation."*

But there was another man named Ananias, who *with his wife Sapphira* sold a piece of land that they owned.

For fear of the people, they brought the apostles back without force.

Him has God raised up with His right hand to be a Prince and a Saviour *in order to give repentance and forgiveness of sins to Israel.*

Discussion

*Why did the early church need so much money?

[Among that great number there were widows and other poor people who needed support. Some of them may have been travelers who stayed at Jerusalem longer than they planned, because of the unusual happenings. The people met for worship every day and needed some means of support.]

Did Ananias and Sapphira have to give all the money?

[No, they could do as they chose. Peter said, "While you had it, was it not your own? And after you sold it, could you not do with it what you wanted?"]

*Why did they want people to think they gave all the money?
[Barnabas had given all his money. Perhaps they wanted the people to praise them for being unselfish.]
Why did the sick people want Peter's shadow to fall on them?
[They probably expected to be healed in this way.]
Why were the captain and officers afraid of the people?
[Many people supported the apostles. If the officers opposed the apostles with force, the people might turn against them and do them harm.]
*Why did Gamaliel think the efforts of Theudas and Judas came to nothing?
[Their programs were only the efforts of men, and not of God.]
Teacher: Note, however, that Gamaliel's reasoning was unsound. The apparent success or failure of an enterprise is **not** a safe guide for determining whether it is of God or of men. What about the widespread success of religions such as those founded many centuries ago by Buddha and Mohammed?

ANSWER KEY

A. 1. d
2. d
3. t
4. d
5. əd
6. əd
7. t
8. t
9. d
10. əd
11. d
12. əd
13. d
14. d
15. d
16. əd
17. t
18. t
19. əd
20. d

B. 1. t
2. s
3. f
4. h
5. gh
6. ie
7. ie
8. five

C. 1. f
2. e
3. c
4. b
5. a
6. d

D. 1. by selling things
2. Levi
3. some land
4. by lying about it
5. after
6. fear
7. Peter's
8. because believers were added to the church
9. an angel
10. to go preach in the temple
11. those who obey God
12. Pharisee
13. of men
14. beat
15. rejoicing

E. 1. Galilee
2. Samaria
3. Judea
4. Nazareth
5. Jerusalem
6. Mediterranean Sea
7. Sea of Galilee
8. Jordan River
9. Dead Sea

LESSON 5
The Witness of Stephen

Oral Reading

Are the children prepared to read the list of names correctly? Encourage practice and clear pronunciation.

Note the pattern of quotation marks. Explain that when one person continues speaking several paragraphs, we indicate his discourse with quotation marks at the beginning of each paragraph, but we use no end quotation marks until he stops speaking.

Quiz

Have the students number their papers from 1 to 15 and write the words for the blanks in the sentences you say.

(widows)   1. The Greek-speaking Jews were unhappy because their _____ were neglected.

(seven)   2. The brethren were told to find _____ men among themselves who were honest and full of the Holy Ghost and wisdom.

(hands)   3. When they had prayed, the apostles laid their _____ on the chosen men to ordain them.

(blasphemy) 4. Some men said of Stephen, "We have heard him speak _____ against Moses and against God."

(an angel)   5. The men in the council saw that Stephen's face looked like the face of _____ .

(Abraham)   6. Stephen began his message with the story of _____ in Mesopotamia.

(patriarchs) 7. Jacob had twelve sons, called the twelve _____ .

(Egypt)   8. Pharaoh made Joseph ruler over _____ .

(boys)   9. Another Pharaoh had the Israelites' baby _____ cast out.

(three)   10. Moses was cared for in his father's house _____ months.

(slavery)   11. Moses though his people should understand that he would deliver them from _____ .

(Midian)   12. After Moses killed an Egyptian, he fled to the land of _____ .

(bush)   13. After Moses was in the wilderness forty years, the Lord appeared to him in a flame of fire in a _____ .

(shoes)   14. God told Moses to take off his _____ .

(Red Sea)   15. Moses led the children of Israel through the _____ and in the wilderness for forty years.

ANSWER KEY

A. 1. Parmenas   5. Timon   **B.** 1. b   4. b
2. Nicanor   6. Stephen   2. c   5. a
3. Nicolas   7. Philip   3. a   6. c
4. Prochorus

7. b	11. c	3. (Line from Ur to Haran)
8. a	12. a	4. (Line from Haran to Canaan)
9. c	13. a	5. (Box around *Egypt*)
10. b	14. c	6. (Dotted line from Egypt to Mount Sinai)
	15. b	

C. 1. c   5. c

    2. a   6. a   *E.*   2

    3. b   7. b   6

    4. a   8. c   4

D.   1. (Mediterranean and Dead   1

      Seas colored blue)   3

    2. (Babylon circled)   5

LESSON 6
Samaria Receives the Word of God

Oral Reading

Are the children maintaining carefulness in reading exactly what appears on the page?

Discussion

*What is the meaning of this sentence: "They killed the ones who foretold the coming of the Just One, whom you have now betrayed and murdered"?

[The forefathers of the Jews killed the prophets who told of Jesus' coming, and the Jews betrayed and murdered Jesus when He came.]

What did Stephen mean when he said, "Lord, do not hold this sin against them"?

[He wanted God to forgive them for killing him.]

What did the believers of Jerusalem do when they were persecuted?

[They scattered everywhere, preaching the Word.]

*What had Jesus told the disciples to do just before He went to heaven?

[He said they should be witnesses to Him in Jerusalem, and in Judea, and in Samaria, and to the uttermost part of the earth.]

*What did Peter mean when he said, "I see that you are in the gall of bitterness"?

[Gall is a bitter fluid formed by the liver. The word may be used for other things that are bitter. Peter was describing Simon's life as a bitter experience because he was turning away from God, as Deuteronomy 29:18 warns against.]

Note: The King James Version says that Simon had "bewitched" the Samaritans. The reader story uses *amazed*, which is a better translation of the Greek word for today's usage.

ANSWER KEY

A.
1. d
2. e
3. f
4. g
5. c
6. h
7. b
8. a
9. j
10. i

B. (Probable answers, if taken from the reader)
1. kept looking up
2. together
3. in favor of
4. sincere and religious
5. very great destruction
6. magic
7. looked up to / honored
8. see

C.
1. 1 (Resisting the Holy Ghost, betraying and murdering Jesus, and not keeping the Law)
2. 2 (Jesus)
3. 3, 4, or 5 (He was stoned.)
4. 4 ("Lord, do not hold this sin against them.")
5. X
6. X
7. 7 (Sincere and religious men)
8. 5 (Saul)
9. 6 (Because of a great persecution)
10. X
11. 9 (The city of Samaria)
12. 9 (Casting out unclean spirits, healing many who were lame or had palsy)
13. 10 (One who did great wonders)
14. 10 (With the help of evil spirits)
15. X
16. X
17. 13 (Peter and John)
18. 13 (Through the laying on of the apostles' hands)
19. 14 (To lay hands on people so that they might receive the Holy Ghost)
20. X
21. X
22. 17 (Through many Samaritan villages as they went toward Jerusalem)
23. 17 (Preached the Gospel)
24. X
25. X

D.
1. The *prophets* foretold the coming of the Just One.
2. The *fathers* of the Jews killed the prophets.
3. The council betrayed and murdered *Jesus*.
4. Stephen's last desire was, *"Lord, do not hold this sin against them."*
5. Saul *kept the clothes* of the ones who stoned Stephen. (or) Saul was *in favor* of Stephen's death.
6. Saul *persecuted* the church.
7. The people were scattered because of the *persecution*, and they preached as they went.
8. *Philip* went to Samaria and preached.

LESSON 7
Conversions of the Ethiopian and Saul

Oral Reading
Challenge the children to detect mistakes as you read passages with little mistakes such as saying *to* for *toward, of* for *from, the* for *this,* and so forth.

Discussion
Where was the Ethiopian man traveling?
[He was on the road from Jerusalem to Gaza, on his way back to Ethiopia.]
Why was Philip along that road?
[The angel of the Lord told him to go there.]
*Which of the two do you think first started on his journey?
[If Philip walked from Samaria—north of Jerusalem—and the Ethiopian traveled southwest from Jerusalem in his chariot, Philip probably started on his journey first.]
Can you answer the Ethiopian's question? Of whom was the prophet speaking "as a lamb before the shearers"?
[The prophet was speaking of Jesus.]
*What is the meaning of the saying, "It is hard for you to kick against the pricks"?
[Pricks are long rods with sharp points on the end. They were used to guide oxen by pricking them from behind. If an animal kicked against this guidance, it only got hurt more. Saul was hurting himself by resisting God's way.]
Who told Saul what he should do?
[The Lord told him to go into the city where he would be told what to do. There it was men like Ananias who told him what to do.]

ANSWER KEY

A. *People* (Any twelve)

Augustus (1)	Caiaphas (3)
Tiberius (1)	Pontus (3)
Claudius (1)	Barnabas (4)
Jesus (1, 6)	Ananias (4)
Alphaeus (1)	Theudas (4)
Judas (1, 4)	Prochorus (5)
Barsabas (1)	Parmenas (5)
Matthias (1)	Nicolas (5)
Annas (3)	

Places

Cyprus (4)	Damascus (7)
Azotus (7)	Tarsus (7)

B.

1. P		12. P	
2. A		13. A	
3. P		14. P	
4. A		15. A	
5. P		16. A	
6. P		17. P	
7. A		18. A	
8. A		19. P	
9. P		20. P	
10. A		21. A	
11. P			

C. 1. Candace
2. The Ethiopian
3. Isaiah

4. Philip
5. The Ethiopian
6. Philip, the Ethiopian
7. Philip
8. Saul
9. Jesus
10. Ananias

12. near
13. others were with him
14. he prayed
15. yes
16. yes
17. yes
18. he preached

D.
1. the angel
2. dry
3. honest
4. Ethiopia
5. Old Testament
6. aloud
7. the Spirit
8. no
9. Jesus Christ
10. happy
11. the Spirit

E.
1. south, Jerusalem, Gaza (Blue line from Samaria, most likely through Jerusalem and for some distance toward Gaza)
2. Azotus, Caesarea
3. Azotus, Jamnia, Joppa, Apollonia, Caesarea
4. Damascus (Red line on most direct road from Jerusalem to Damascus—probably through Bethany)

LESSON 8
Gentiles Receive the Holy Ghost

Oral Reading

Observe commas as signs for a short pause. Commas help divide sentences into meaningful phrases. Demonstrate with these sentences.

She opened her eyes, and when she saw Peter, she sat up.

Giving her his hand, Peter lifted her up; and when he had called the saints and widows, he presented her alive.

Discussion

Why did Saul leave Damascus?

[The Jews there were watching for a chance to kill him.]

Why did Saul leave Jerusalem?

[The Greek-speaking Jews there were planning to kill him.]

*Why does the story say the brethren took Saul *down* to Caesarea from Jerusalem?

[Jerusalem is on a mountain. We are accustomed to saying *up* north and *down* south, but in these accounts people traveled up to Jerusalem and down to Damascus.]

Trace Peter's travel on a map. (See general plan for this unit.)

[Lydda, Joppa, Caesarea]

Why did Peter object to eating what was before him in the vision?

[The animals he saw were unclean according to the Jewish law.]

What did the unclean animals in the vision represent in real life?

[They represented the Gentile people, whom the Jews considered unclean.]

What was the vision supposed to teach Peter?

[God would cleanse the Gentiles and accept them as well as the Jews.]

What convinced Peter and the Jews with him that God had accepted the Gentiles as well as the Jews?

[The Holy Ghost was given to the Gentiles as Peter preached.]

Workbook Notes

To avoid confusion in part G, tell the students to first number all the sentences that relate to Cornelius and then the sentences that relate to Peter.

You may want to give some help in finding distance on a map with a scale of miles for numbers 4 and 5 in part H. Lay the edge of a paper along the scale of miles and mark dots at ten-mile intervals. Then lay that paper on the map along the distance to be measured.

ANSWER KEY

A.
1. vision
2. religious
3. escaped
4. increased
5. relatives
6. tanner
7. widows
8. instructed
9. declared
10. requesting

B. (Any four)
Damascus
Aeneas
Jesus
Dorcas
Cornelius

C.
1. b
2. e
3. d
4. c
5. a

D.
1. Saul
2. Barnabas
3. Peter
4. Aeneas
5. Dorcas
6. Simon
7. Cornelius

E.
8. Damascus
9. Jerusalem
10. Tarsus
11. Joppa
12. Lydda
13. Caesarea

F.
14. eight
15. three
16. four
17. three

G.
3
2
4
3
2
1
4
5
1
5

H. 1. southwest
    2. northwest
    3. He probably went by ship.
    4. ten miles

5. thirty miles
6. Mediterranean Sea
7. Simon
8. north

LESSON 9
Peter's Release From Prison

Oral Reading

Is there a proper speed in oral reading? When the other aspects are well mastered, there is a greater tendency to read too fast than too slowly. Demonstrate a reading speed that makes it easy for listeners to get the most from a story.

Discussion

Why did the Jews object to what Peter had done at Caesarea?
    [They did not think it was right to eat with Gentiles.]
What satisfied the Jews that the Gentiles were also accepted by God?
    [They were satisfied when they heard Peter's account of his vision and the gift of the Holy Ghost to the Gentiles.]
How did Barnabas come to be at Antioch?
    [The church at Jerusalem sent him when they heard there were believers at Antioch.]
How did Saul come to be at Antioch?
    [Barnabas went to Tarsus to find Saul and brought him to Antioch.]
Why did Barnabas and Saul go to Judea?
    [They carried relief for the brethren suffering from the famine there.]
How did Peter get out of prison?
    [An angel woke him, his chains fell off, and the gate opened of its own accord.]
*What were the Jews expecting to happen to Peter?
    [They probably expected him to be killed.]
Why did the people at Mary's house think Rhoda was beside herself?
    [They did not think Peter could be out of prison, and Rhoda said he was at the door.]
    Note: In the King James Version, Acts 11:19 says that the believers preached the Gospel in "Phenice." This was not Phenice (Phoenix) on the island of Crete, but the land of Phoenicia in northern Palestine. The reader story uses *Phoenicia*.

ANSWER KEY

A. 1. alms
2. devout
3. bedfast
4. cleansed
5. oppose
6. urged
7. famine
8. relief
9. arrested
10. ceasing
11. departed
12. beckoned

5. astonished
7. Tarsus
10. Agabus
11. John
12. Mary
13. side
14. baptized
15. street
18. iron
19. chains
21. vision
24. city
26. two

B.   *Across*
4. Caesarea
6. hit
8. keep
9. beasts
11. James
14. Barnabas
15. Saul
16. Herod
17. persecution
20. sixteen
22. Antioch
23. trance
25. determination
27. Rhoda
28. angel

Down
1. gate
2. Joppa
3. voice

C. 1. a. James
b. James
2. a. Simon
b. Simon
3. a. Ananias
b. Ananias
4. a. Mary
b. Mary

D. 1. b   7. c
2. c   8. c
3. b   9. b
4. a   10. b
5. b   11. a
6. a   12. c

E. (Three lines from Jerusalem—to Phoenicia, Cyprus, and Antioch)

Gradebook: 66 points

LESSON 10
Paul and Barnabas as Missionaries

Oral Reading

Consider the volume of oral reading. Use a loud tone for the shout of the people when they exalted Herod. Lower the voice for the parenthetical phrase referring to Saul's change of name. When Paul addressed the congregation in the synagogue, he likely raised his voice to be heard by all.

Discussion

*How do you think Herod examined the keepers of the prison?

[He asked them questions about Peter's escape.]

Why did he have the keepers put to death?

[He considered them responsible for letting Peter get away.]

Why was Herod stricken by the angel?

[He took praise to himself and did not glorify God.]

What was the work of Barnabas and Saul at Jerusalem?

[Lesson 9 says they were sent to Judea with relief from Antioch.]

Why was Elymas smitten with blindness?

[He tried to turn Sergius Paulus away from the faith.]

Trace the journeys of Paul and Barnabas on a map.

[Jerusalem, Antioch, Seleucia, Cyprus (Salamis and Paphos), Perga, Antioch in Pisidia]

How many Old Testament men can you name whom Paul mentioned in his message?

[Samuel, Saul, Kish, Benjamin, David, Jesse, Abraham, Moses]

ANSWER KEY

A.
1. mischief
2. fasted
3. decay
4. sought
5. stir
6. examined
7. converted
8. subtlety
9. congregation
10. tidings
11. deputy
12. sepulcher

B.
1. (Any order)
   Cornelius, Aeneas, Agabus, Candace, Sergius Paulus, Bar-jesus, Elymas
2. (Any order)

Antioch	Tarsus
Caesarea	Lydda
Seleucia	Sidon
Saron	Paphos
Azotus	Perga
Tyre	Damascus
Salamis	

3. (Any order)
   Syria
   Pamphylia
   Mesopotamia
   Ethiopia
   Pisidia

C.

4	2	6
5	1	3

D.
1. A soldier could *lose his life* for letting a prisoner escape.
2. Herod was eaten by worms because he *did not give God the glory.*
3. Barnabas and Saul took *relief* from Antioch for the brethren in Judea.
4. *John Mark* went along on the missionary journey.
5. John Mark *left Barnabas and Paul* at Perga and returned to Jerusalem.

6. A sorcerer does *magic* through the power of evil spirits.
7. Saul was also called *Paul.*
8. *David* was a man after God's own heart.
9. *David's body decayed,* but *Jesus was raised* again.

E. (Check the map on pages 48 and 49 for the following points.)
1. Cyprus colored yellow
2. Pamphylia colored light orange
3. Pisidia colored pink or light red
4. Green line connecting—
Antioch in Syria
Seleucia
Salamis
Paphos
Perga
Antioch in Pisidia

LESSON 11
Paul and Barnabas Continue Their Ministry

Oral Reading
Encourage clear, loud reading that could be easily heard by an audience.

Discussion
Why did the Jews contradict what Paul said?
[They were envious because people were so eager to hear him.]
Why did the Jews stir up persecution against Paul and Barnabas?
[They were displeased because many Gentiles believed and the Word of God was published through all that region.]
*Why did Paul and Barnabas shake the dust off their feet when they left Antioch?
[They were following the directions of Jesus, given in Matthew 10:14; Mark 6:11; and Luke 9:5. This was a testimony against the people of Antioch because they refused the Word of God.]
Why did Paul and Barnabas leave Iconium?
[The people there tried to harm the apostles and stone them.]
How did the people at Lystra receive Paul and Barnabas at first?
[They thought they were gods and prepared to sacrifice to them.]
What changed the people's minds?
[Some Jews came from Antioch and Iconium and turned the people against them.]
Why did Paul and Barnabas leave Lystra?
[The people had stoned Paul and thought he was dead.]
Did Paul ever go back to Lystra?
[Yes, they returned to Lystra, Iconium, and Antioch to encourage the believers there.]

Continue tracing the journeys of Paul and Barnabas on a map.
[Antioch in Pisidia, Iconium, Lystra, Derbe, Lystra, Iconium, Antioch in P., Perga, Attalia, Antioch in Syria. After the missionary journey, they went through Phoenicia and Samaria to Jerusalem to settle a question with the elders.]

ANSWER KEY

A.
1. b (The rest mean groups.)
2. a (The rest name self-exalting attitudes.)
3. c (The rest mean speaking.)
4. a (The rest express agreement.)
5. d (The rest speak of bearing news.)
6. b (The rest name hardships.)
7. c (The rest speak of special callings.)
8. b (The rest name buildings of worship.)
9. a (The rest speak of pushing opinion.)

B. (Possible answers)
1. *cattle*—animals of the cow family
2. *unworthy*—not deserving
3. *determination*—strong purpose of mind
4. *contradict*—say the opposite; disagree
5. *invented*—made something not known before
6. *energy*—strength
7. *forbidden*—not allowed
8. *pasture*—meadow; field of grass
9. *committed*—given to the trust of another

C.
1. Sabbath
2. Jews
3. envy
4. Paul
5. bold
6. necessary
7. Gentiles
8. cripple
9. born
10. faith
11. stoned
12. dead
13. taught
14. souls
15. faith
16. tribulation
17. Antioch
18. Jew(s)
19. Gentile(s)
20. faith

D. (Check the map on pages 48 and 49.)

Green line continued from Antioch in Pisidia to Iconium, Lystra, Derbe, Lystra, Iconium, Antioch, Perga, Attalia, Antioch in Syria

E.
1. d
2. e
3. f
4. c
5. a
6. g
7. j
8. b
9. h
10. i

LESSON 12
The Meeting at Jerusalem

Oral Reading

Encourage careful enunciation, sounding every syllable clearly.

Discussion

Why did Paul and his companions go to Jerusalem?

[They wanted to settle the question about keeping the Old Testament Law.]

How did they settle the problem?

[They discussed it with the apostles and elders. Each had a turn to speak
in an orderly manner, and they came to an agreement.]

What problem did Paul and Barnabas have when they wanted to visit the
churches again?

[They could not agree about taking John Mark along.]

How did they solve that problem?

[They traveled separately, each taking another person with him.]

What problem did Paul and Silas have when they wanted to preach in
Bithynia?

[Their plan did not agree with the Spirit's plan for them.]

How did they solve that problem?

[They gave up their own ideas and went somewhere else.]

*When Peter spoke, what did he mean by the yoke that their fathers could
not bear?

[The requirements of the Law were a heavy burden that they could not
keep perfectly.]

Trace Paul's travels on a map.

[Return to Antioch from Jerusalem conference. Second missionary journey: Antioch in S., through Cilicia, Derbe, Lystra, Iconium, Antioch in
P., through Phrygia, across Asia to Mysia, Troas]

Workbook Note

For the map exercise in part F, "all the cities where we have preached"
includes Antioch in Pisidia which is not named in this lesson.

ANSWER KEY

A.			B. (Possible answers)
1. h	10. q		1. near
2. f	11. n		2. going up
3. g	12. r		3. alive
4. a	13. o		4. hindered
5. b	14. j		5. end
6. i	15. l		6. gathered
7. d	16. k		7. last name
8. c	17. p		
9. e	18. m		

C. (Misused homophones by lines)
they're, bin
no
cent, two
too
(No errors in fifth line)
there, harts, buy, due
yolk, hour
wee, bare, threw
bee
(Correct words)

there	by
been	do
know	yoke
sent	our
to	we
to	bear
their	through
hearts	be

D. 1. the apostles and elders and brethren

2. the Gentile brethren
3. from Jerusalem
4. Barnabas, Paul, Judas, and Silas
5. for the Name of Jesus
6. eating meat offered to idols
   eating blood
   eating things strangled
   fornication

E.
1. b	6. c
2. a	7. b
3. c	8. a
4. a	9. b
5. a	10. c

F. (Check the map on pages 48 and 49.)

A purple line from Antioch in S., through Cilicia, to Derbe, Lystra, Iconium, Antioch in P., through Phrygia, across Asia to Mysia, Troas

LESSON 13
The Philippian Jailer

Oral Reading

Let oral expression convey the urgency of the appeal of the Macedonian in Paul's vision, show Paul's displeasure when he rebuked the spirit of divination, and show the excitement of the earthquake and the open prison.

Discussion

How did God show Paul where He wanted him to go?
[He sent him a vision in the night.]
Whom did Paul and Silas help in Macedonia?
[The women who prayed at the riverside, Lydia and her household, the jailer and his household, and many people in the various cities where they preached.]
Who was it that did not receive help?
[The Jews who did not believe did not receive help.]
Who set the city in an uproar at Thessalonica?
[The envious Jews gathered a crowd of wicked men who set the city in an uproar.]

What did the Jews accuse Paul and Silas of doing?

[They said that these men had turned the world upside down and that they contradicted the laws of Caesar.]

Trace Paul's travels on a map.

[Troas, toward Samothracia, Neapolis, Philippi, Amphipolis, Apollonia, Thessalonica, Berea]

ANSWER KEY

A.

1. b	6. a	11. no	16. yes
2. c	7. c	12. yes	17. yes
3. c	8. c	13. no	18. yes
4. a	9. a	14. yes	19. no
5. b	10. b	15. yes	20. no

B.
1. questioned
2. inquired
3. instructed
4. thought
5. shouted
6. warned
7. cried
8. urged
9. pleaded
10. declared

C.

1. yes	6. yes
2. yes	7. no
3. no	8. no
4. no	9. yes
5. yes	10. no

D. (Possible answers)
1. A Christian woman from Thyatira who was a seller of purple at Philippi
2. A disciple at Thessalonica who lodged Paul and Silas

E. (Check the map on pages 48 and 49.)

Purple line from Troas to Neapolis (curving toward Samothracia), Philippi, Amphipolis, Apollonia, Thessalonica, Berea

LESSON 14
Paul Preaches on Mars' Hill

Oral Reading

In a passage such as Paul's sermon, emphasize good enunciation fitting for addressing an audience.

Discussion

How were the Jews of Berea more noble than those in Thessalonica?

[They checked the Scriptures on the things Paul said, and they were ready to believe the truth.]

How were the people of Berea stirred up against Paul?

[Jews from Thessalonica came to make trouble for Paul.]

How did Paul get to Athens?

[Some men escorted him there because of the trouble at Berea.]

What was the custom of the people in Athens?

[They spent their time telling and hearing new things.]

What did they think was strange about Paul's teaching?

[They thought the resurrection of the dead was a strange teaching.]

Why did Paul shake out his clothes at Corinth?

[This was probably a form of shaking off the dust as a response to their rejection of his teaching.]

ANSWER KEY

A.
1. bedfast
2. seaside
3. housetop
4. four-footed
5. riverside
6. marketplace
7. earthquake
8. tentmakers

B.
1. Bereans
2. escorts
3. jailer
4. tanner
5. relatives
6. prisoner

C.
1. d
2. f
3. a
4. h
5. j
6. g
7. c
8. b
9. l
10. k
11. i
12. e

D. (Possible answers)
1. A Christian tentmaker who lived at Corinth
2. The wife of Aquila
3. The ruler of the synagogue at Corinth who became a Christian
4. A disciple at Corinth

E.
1. c
2. a
3. b
4. c

F.
I. A. The one they called Unknown
B. Creator of the world
C. Lord of heaven and earth

II. A. Desire to seek the Lord
B. Live and move and have being in Him
C. Ignorance overlooked in the past
D. Repentance required

III. A. Judgment by Him
B. Raised from the dead

G. (Check the map on pages 48 and 49.)

Purple line from Berea to Athens and Corinth

LESSON 15
Disciples at Ephesus

Oral Reading

Use expression fitting to the Jews' hostility, the deputy's scorn, the Ephesian disciples' innocence, and the vagabond Jews' presumption and disaster.

Quiz

After oral reading, give the students opportunity to list on paper all the places they can think of which Paul visited in this lesson, without referring to the reader or a map. Then have them consider the names they recalled and rewrite or number them in the order they think he traveled to them.

Give ten points for each name and one additional point for each name in correct order. (A fourth-grader who lists all ten names in correct order deserves 110%!)

Corinth
Cenchrea
Ephesus
Syria
Caesarea
Jerusalem
Antioch
Galatia
Phrygia
Ephesus

Discussion

How did Aquila and Priscilla happen to be at Ephesus when Apollos was teaching there?

[They had traveled with Paul from Corinth to Ephesus, and Paul left them there.]

ANSWER KEY

A.		
1. a	13. a	25. a
2. b	14. b	26. b
3. a	15. a	27. b
4. b	16. b	
5. a	17. b	
6. b	18. a	
7. b	19. b	
8. a	20. a	
9. a	21. a	
10. b	22. b	
11. a	23. b	
12. b	24. a	

28. a
29. b
30. a

B.		
1. dew	9. noon
2. dough	10. known
3. set	11. comb
4. seat	12. came
5. low	13. wind
6. law	14. wound
7. speak	15. wrote
8. speck	16. root

17. greet
18. great
19. talk
20. take
21. feel
22. fell
23. miss

24. mice
25. fox
26. folks
27. pressed
28. priest
29. chilled
30. child

had seven sons who worked magic

D.

3	6	12	19	23
5	10	11	18	21
1	9	15	17	25
2	8	14	16	22
4	7	13	20	24

C.
1. A ruler of the synagogue at Corinth who was beaten by the Greeks
2. A Jew from Alexandria to whom Aquila and Priscilla taught the way of God more perfectly
3. A man who had a school at Ephesus
4. A Jewish chief priest who

E.   (Check the map on pages 48 and 49.)
1. Purple line from Corinth to Cenchrea, Ephesus, Caesarea, Jerusalem, Antioch
2. Black line from Antioch through Galatia (Derbe, Lystra, Iconium, Antioch) and Phrygia, Ephesus

LESSON 16
The Uproar at Ephesus

Oral Reading

There is an abundance of irritation and turmoil in this story. Read it expressively.

Discussion

What do you think was the greatest concern of Demetrius?

[He was probably upset because he would be losing money.]

What stirred up most of the people in the uproar?

[They were stirred up by the confusion and shouting.]

What reasons did the town clerk give against the uproar?

[There was no question about the worship of Diana. These men had not done anything against the Ephesians' worship. The silversmiths should have taken care of their problem in a lawful way.]

*One of the disciples who sailed to Troas to travel with Paul was Gaius. Was he the same man who was caught and taken into the theater with Aristarchus?

[No, the one caught in the uproar at Ephesus was a Macedonian. The Gaius who sailed to Troas was from Derbe.]

Workbook Note

In marking the map for part F, the children should include the cities touched on the journeys, though not specifically named in the story.

ANSWER KEY

A.
1. (är•is•tär' kus)
2. (as' əs)
3. (kī' əs)
4. (dē•mē' tri•us)
5. (ē•ras' tus)
6. (ū' tē•kus)
7. (gā' us)
8. (mī•lē' tus)
9. (mit' ə•lē' nē)
10. (sā' məs)
11. (sē•kun' dus)
12. (sō' pa•tər)
13. (trō' əs)
14. (trō•jil' ē•um)
15. (trof' i•mus)
16. (tik' i•kus)

B. *People*

Aristarchus
Demetrius
Erastus
Eutychus
Gaius
Secundus
Sopater
Trophimus
Tychicus

Places

Assos
Chios
Miletus
Mitylene
Samos
Troas
Trogyllium

C.
1. c   6. h
2. e   7. d
3. g   8. b
4. i   9. f
5. a   10. j

D.
1. two
2. silversmith
3. something for her
4. others also
5. many others
6. Macedonia
7. not know
8. Alexander
9. two hours
10. Jupiter
11. unnecessary
12. first day
13. all night
14. three
15. by ship
16. on foot
17. Paul
18. travel every day

E.
1. Judas
2. Ananias
3. Simon
4. Masters of a girl
5. Demetrius

F. (Check the map on pages 48 and 49.)

Black line from Ephesus to Macedonia (Philippi, Amphipolis, Apollonia, Thessalonica, Berea), Greece (Athens, Corinth), return to Philippi, Troas, Assos, Mitylene, by Chios, Trogyllium, Miletus

LESSON 17
Paul's Address to the Ephesian Elders

Oral Reading

Give attention to careful pronunciation of names and multi-syllable words.

Discussion

*Why did Paul think the Ephesian elders would not see him again?
[He expected bonds and afflictions would come to him and he would no longer travel around to visit the churches.]
*What grievous wolves was Paul talking about?
[He was speaking of false teachers who would do harm to the church.]
What other danger did he warn the leaders of?
[He said men in the church would rise and speak wicked things to draw away followers.]
*Do you remember any other prophecies made by Agabus?
[He foretold the famine that came in the days of Claudius Caesar.]
What do you think was going to happen to Paul at Jerusalem?
[The prophecy indicates that he faced imprisonment.]
*Why didn't Paul change his mind about going to Jerusalem?
[He was willing to face bonds and death and felt it was the Lord's will for him to go on.]
*What did the elders at Jerusalem suggest in hopes that the Jews would feel kindly toward Paul?
[They asked him to join some brethren in the observance of a vow according to the Law.]

ANSWER KEY

A.
1. Pentecost
2. humility
3. personally
4. affliction
5. publicly
6. declared
7. indicates
8. testify
9. overseers
10. grievous
11. inheritance
12. evangelist
13. lodge
14. vow
15. strangled
16. observance

B.
1. wind (wine)
2. "they (delete quotation marks)
3. sliver (silver)
4. indent (intend)
5. Down (lower-case *d*)
6. four, (comma should be hyphen)
7. thinks (things)
8. ? (.)
9. trail (trial)
10. pentecost (capital *p*)

C.
1. The *church* was the flock.
2. *False teachers* were the grievous wolves.
3. a. Labor to *support the weak*.
   b. Labor to have things to *give*.
4. They wept most of all because they would *not see Paul again*.
5. They wanted him to *show that he kept the Jewish customs*.

D. 1. c   6. c   ***E.*** (Check the map on pages 48 and
       2. a   7. b   49.)
       3. b   8. c   Black line from Miletus to
       4. a   9. b   Coos, Rhodes, Patara, south of
       5. a   10. a   Cyprus, Tyre, Ptolemais, Cae-
                               sarea, Jerusalem

LESSON 18
Paul's Address at Jerusalem

Oral Reading

Give a reminder of the purpose for commas and strive for smooth reading with meaningful phrasing.

Discussion

Whom had the Jews seen that made them think Paul was taking Gentiles into the temple?

[They saw Trophimus, an Ephesian, in the city with Paul.]

*Do you remember any references to Trophimus before this?

[Trophimus was one of the disciples listed in lesson 16 who sailed to Troas to travel with Paul.]

What triggered the uproar and arrest of Paul?

[Some Jews saw Paul in the temple and cried out against him.]

What kept Paul from being killed?

[The chief captain interfered and took Paul prisoner.]

What triggered the outbreak again when Paul was making his defense before the people?

[The people cried out against him when he mentioned the Gentiles.]

ANSWER KEY

A. 1. foolish, excited
       2. confused, quick
       3. rude, unkind, unwise
       4. mean, rough
       5. fast, angry, noisy
       6. courteous, obedient
       7. cautious, worried
       8. quiet, attentive
       9. unkind, stirred up
      10. joyful, submissive
      11. guilty, sorry
      12. loving, peaceful, joyful

      13. surprised, curious
      14. interested, diligent

B. *People*
      Aeneas (8)
      Dorcas (8)
      Cornelius (8)
      Agabus (9, 17)
      Bar-jesus (10)
      Elymas (10)
      Sergius Paulus (10)
      Silas (12, 13, 14)
      Justus (14)

Crispus (14)
Apollos (15)
Tyrannus (15)
Erastus (16)
Demetrius (16)
Gaius (16)
Aristarchus (16)
Secundus (16)
Tychicus (16)
Trophimus (16)
Eutychus (16)
Places
Paphos (10)
Troas (12, 16)
Pontus (14)
Ephesus (15, 16, 17)
Assos (16)
Chios (16)
Samos (16)
Miletus (16, 17)
Coos (17)

C. (Possible answers)
1. A disciple from Ephesus who traveled with Paul
2. A Jewish teacher of the Law at Jerusalem

D. (The numbers to the left side of the design tell which questions pertain to each row. Italicized numbers are questions that would mar the pattern.)

2, 13, *14*
12, 21
3, 5, *9*
16, *18*
10, 15
4, 8
19
7, 17
6, 11, 20
1

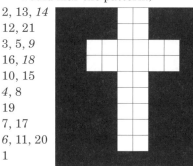

E. 1. the Holy Ghost
2. new wine
3. wonder, amazement
4. love
5. Satan
6. faith, power, the Holy Ghost
7. good works, almsdeeds
8. subtlety, mischief
9. envy
10. joy
11. anger
12. confusion

LESSON 19
Paul Is Taken to Caesarea

Oral Reading

Use expression to bring out the feeling of the conversation and actions in the story.

Discussion

*What is a whited wall?

[A whited wall is coated with whitewash to make it look attractive, but underneath the coating, the wall is plain stone or brick, and may not look beautiful at all.]

*Why did Paul call Ananias a whited wall?

[On the outside Ananias appeared to be a godly man, but inside he was not godly. Paul realized he was a hypocrite and used this comparison to tell him so.]

Why did the turmoil arise in the Jewish council?

[Paul brought up the subject of the resurrection, on which the Pharisees and Sadducees disagreed.]

How was Paul spared from the death which the Jews planned?

[His sister's son heard of the plan and reported it. The chief captain had Paul sent away in the night with a band of soldiers.]

Where was Paul sent?

[He was sent to Caesarea to be judged by the governor there.]

Trace Paul's travels on a map.

[Jerusalem, Antipatris, Caesarea]

ANSWER KEY

A.

1. 2	4. 5	7. 5
3	3	3
5	2	1
4	4	2
1	1	4

2. 2	5. 1	8. 1
5	2	2
4	5	5
3	3	3
1	4	4

3. 1	6. 3	9. 3
4	1	1
2	4	5
5	2	4
3	5	2

B.
1. good
2. whited
3. following
4. forty
5. great
6. chief
7. young
8. seventy
9. excellent
10. judgment

C.

4	9	15	18
2	7	11	16
1	10	12	19
3	8	13	17
5	6	14	20

D.
1. He wanted to know *why the Jews accused* Paul.
2. The Pharisees believed in the *resurrection*. The Sadducees did not believe in the resurrection.
3. God told Paul *he would testify at Rome.*
4. *Paul* was bound with chains or ropes.
5. *Forty Jews* were bound by a sworn promise.

E.
1. c	3. c	6. a
2. a	4. a	7. b
	5. c	

F. (Check the map on pages 48 and 49.)

Red line from Jerusalem to Antipatris and Caesarea

Gradebook: 59 points, counting one point for each word group in part A, and two points for each sentence in part D.

LESSON 20
Paul Before Felix and Festus

Oral Reading

Check the volume of oral reading. Do the children need a reminder to speak up?

Discussion

*Why do you think Tertullus began his speech the way he did?

[He began by praising Felix and his rule. This was probably to make Felix favor him and the things he had to say.]

*Why would it cheer Paul that Felix had been the governor for many years?

[Having governed for many years, Felix would know a good deal about the ways and laws of the Jews.]

What did Paul say were the things for which he might be accused?

[He worshiped God in a way the Jews called heresy, and he started the uproar in the Jewish council.]

*Why do you think Felix trembled?

[He was not saved, and he feared the judgment to come.]

How did the Jews feel about Paul by the time two years had passed?

[They were still looking for a chance to kill him.]

ANSWER KEY

A.
1. d
2. f
3. a
4. g
5. b
6. e
7. c
8. h
9. l
10. k
11. j
12. i

B. (Explanation of difference may vary.)
1. Tertullus—names a man; the others are cities.
2. Macedonia—names a land; the others are men.
3. against—describes a position; the others refer to speaking.
4. rudeness—is unkind treatment; the others are virtues.
5. Jerusalem—names a city; the others are lands.
6. Pentecost—names a feast; the others are buildings.
7. since—describes relationship of time; the others are measures.
8. liberty—is a state of being; the others can be monetary.
9. rooster—is a bird; the others are four-footed.
10. horse—is an animal; the others are vehicles.

C. (Phrases to be crossed out)
2. After many days
3. After some days
6. Ten days or more
7. For many years
10. Very worthy deeds
12. A certain man
14. About a certain question
15. Liberty to bring him things
17. Religious discussion

D.
1. Tertullus
2. Lysias
3. Drusilla
4. Ananias
5. Felix
6. Caesar
7. Festus
8. Tarsus
9. Jerusalem
10. Damascus
11. Rome
12. Antioch
13. Joppa
14. Caesarea

E.
1. a. He was a troublesome fellow who *caused rebellion.*
   b. He had tried to *defile the temple.*
2. a. He believed all things written in the *Law and in the prophets.*
   b. He believed in the *resurrection* of the dead.
3. The Jews called that way *heresy.*
4. Felix trembled at the thought of *righteousness, temperance, and judgment.*

LESSON 21
Paul's Address to Agrippa

Oral Reading
   Emphasize the importance of reading correctly. Do not allow any words omitted or added.

Discussion
Why was Festus surprised at Paul's trial?
   [He expected to hear crimes charged against Paul, but the accusations were only about his religion and Jesus.]
What did Festus expect to result from the trial of Paul before Agrippa?
   [He wanted to have something to say about Paul when he was sent to Caesar.]
Did Agrippa know more about the Jews' teaching and lives than Festus knew?
   [Yes, Festus admitted that he did not know about this kind of questions, and Paul spoke of Agrippa's acquaintance with the customs and questions of the Jews.]

Did Agrippa think Paul was worthy of death?

[No, he said Paul might have been set free if he had not appealed to Caesar.]

What did Paul wish for all the people present at the trial?

[He wished they would all be like him, that is, be Christians.]

ANSWER KEY

A.
1. prison
2. accuse
3. judge
4. expect
5. special
6. examine
7. permit
8. believe
9. forgive
10. inherit
11. repent
12. sober

B. (Possible answers)
1. told about Paul's case
2. told me about him and wanted him to be sentenced to death
3. with great splendor
4. my life as a strict Pharisee
5. unbelievable
6. permission and orders

C.
1. Festus
2. Agrippa
3. Festus
4. Agrippa
5. Paul
6. Jesus
7. Paul
8. Festus
9. Agrippa
10. Agrippa

D. (Allow varying order of points within main sections.)

I.
  A. Was a strict Pharisee
  B. Persecuted Jesus and His followers
  C. Put saints in prison
  D. Went to Damascus to persecute

II.
  A. Bright light
  B. Voice
  C. Direction for service

III.
  A. To Jews and Gentiles
  B. Repent and live lives that show repentance

IV.
  A. Was caught by Jews who tried to kill him
  B. Was helped by God
  C. Was still preaching what Moses and the prophets had said

E.
1. a   5. b
2. c   6. a
3. a   7. c
4. b   8. c

LESSON 22
Shipwreck

Oral Reading

Give attention to careful pronunciation of all the names.

Discussion

*Why was sailing dangerous in this season?

[Stormy weather made it unsafe to travel on the sea through the months of winter.]

*How do you think Paul knew that the voyage would bring damage?

[God probably revealed it to him through the Spirit.]

How did Paul know that no one would lose his life although the ship would be destroyed?

[The angel of God told him.]

Why were the sailors afraid when they realized they were near land?

[They were afraid the ship would be wrecked on the rocks.]

What would happen if the prisoners swam out and escaped?

[The soldiers could be killed for letting the prisoners get away.]

Trace Paul's travels on a map.

[Caesarea, Sidon, north of Cyprus, Myra, by the east end of Crete, Fair Havens, south of Clauda, west into the open sea. (The story ends with the ship anchored near unknown land. They were on the coast of Melita.)]

ANSWER KEY

A. (Possible answers)

1. A part of the sea sheltered by land
2. The calm, protected side
3. The goods carried on a ship
4. An object on a rope dropped into the water to keep a ship from moving
5. The back end of a boat
6. A flat piece at the back of the ship that can be turned to steer the ship
7. The largest sail on a sailing ship

B.
1. (a•dra•mit' ē•um)
2. (mī' rə)
3. (lish' ē•ə)
4. (sal•mō' nē)
5. (la•sē' ə)
6. (fē' nis)
7. (klô' də)
8. (ā•drē•at' ik)

C.
1. no
2. no
3. no
4. no
5. yes
6. storms
7. Paul
8. an angel told him
9. closer
10. it was dark
11. fourteen
12. gave thanks
13. two hundred seventy-six
14. the force of the waves

15. some by swimming, some on boards

D. (Individual work. You may want to give the children a chance to identify their classmates' pictures.)

E. 1. b, d, e
   2. b, c

3. a, b

F. (Check the map on pages 48 and 49.)

Red line from Caesarea to Sidon, around the north of Cyprus, Myra, by the east end of Crete, Fair Havens, south of Clauda, west into open sea

LESSON 23
Paul at Rome

Oral Reading

Observe punctuation and proper speed.

Discussion

What made the natives of Melita think Paul was especially wicked?

[He was bitten by a snake, which they took as a sign of God's judgment.]

What made them think he must be a god?

[The snakebite did not harm him.]

*Why did Paul want to talk to the Jewish leaders at Rome?

[He called for them to speak about the hope of Israel. He was eager to convince them that Jesus is the Christ.]

Did the Jews at Rome feel the same way toward Paul as the Jews at Jerusalem did?

[No, they had not received evil reports about him.]

Did the Jews at Rome accept Paul's teaching?

[Some of them believed, and some did not believe.]

*The Bible does not tell about the end of Paul's life. Do you know what happened after the story?

[The emperor Nero sentenced Paul to death several years later, and he was beheaded outside the city of Rome.]

Follow Paul's travels on a map.

[Melita, Syracuse, Rhegium, Puteoli, Appii Forum, Three Taverns, Rome]

Extra Activity

Have the children make riddles with names from Unit 2, giving the first letter of the name and some information about the person. The same thing may be done with names of places.

Let the students share their riddles in class for the others to identify. The glossary will help if the children cannot pull the names from memory.

ANSWER KEY

A. (Order of pairs may vary.)
1. poisonous, venomous
2. coast, shore
3. courteously, kindly
4. comprehend, perceive
5. insensitive, dull

B. *Across*
1. harm
4. coast
8. Publius
9. bit
11. natives
13. disagreed
16. courage
17. two
18. Syracuse
21. Rome
23. letters
25. cold
26. dull
27. Paul
28. escaped

Down
1. hand
2. Melita
3. island
4. courteously
5. snake
6. murderer
7. god
10. winter
12. very
14. Go
15. sea
18. seven
19. customs
20. swell
22. bundle

23. live
24. trip

C. 1. A poisonous *snake bit Paul*, and they thought that was God's judgment.
2. *Paul was not hurt* by the snakebite, which was a miracle.
3. He wanted to talk to them about the *hope of Israel*. (or) He wanted to convince them from the Scripture that *Jesus is the Christ*.

D. 1. the Holy Ghost
2. Barnabas
3. Silas
4. Mary
5. Rhoda
6. Dorcas
7. Lydia
8. Drusilla
9. Eutychus
10. Aquila
11. Priscilla
12. Demetrius
13. Cornelius
14. Simon
15. James
16. Stephen
17. Philip
18. Paul
19. Herod

E. (Check the map on pages 48 and 49.)
Red line to Melita, Syracuse, Rhegium, Puteoli, Appii Forum, Three Taverns, Rome

TEST

ANSWER KEY

A.
1. e	8. m
2. g	9. d
3. c	10. n
4. h	11. i
5. a	12. l
6. b	13. f
7. j	14. k

B.
1. Rome
2. Corinth
3. Philippi
4. Ephesus
5. Tarsus
6. Antioch
7. Damascus
8. Caesarea
9. Jerusalem
10. Melita
11. Crete
12. Cyprus

C.
1. Antioch
2. Caesarea
3. Tarsus
4. Damascus
5. Cyprus
6. Corinth
7. Rome
8. Jerusalem
9. Crete
10. Melita
11. Philippi
12. Ephesus

D.
1. Eutychus
2. Cornelius
3. Agabus
4. Aquila
5. Demetrius
6. Apollos
7. Barnabas
8. Gamaliel
9. Ananias
10. Candace
11. Lydia
12. Aristarchus

Gradebook: 50 test points

Unit Three

Job, Psalms, Proverbs

UNIT 3
General Plan

Unit 3 is based on the poetical books of the Bible, including five lessons from Job, ten lessons from Psalms, and fifteen lessons from Proverbs.

The Psalms section is in poetry form. Many of these poems can be sung by matching the meter to that of familiar tunes. Some suitable tunes are mentioned in the daily lesson plans.

The Proverbs section is a collection of stories that illustrate the Proverb at the beginning of each lesson. You may want to include these Proverbs in your Bible memory program.

The unit test in the back of the pupil's workbook should be removed and filed before the workbooks are distributed.

Unit 3   Lessons

LESSON 1
Job's Affliction

Oral Reading
    Review the standards of posture and book holding for oral reading. Standing straight and holding the book right will subconsciously influence a person to read clearly and expressively.

Discussion
Where did Job live?
    [Job lived in the land of Uz.]
Describe Job's character.
    [He was perfectly upright. He feared God and avoided everything evil.]
*In what ways was Job a great man?
    [He was great in character. He was great in material possessions.]
Why did Job pray for his children?
    [He realized that they might be tempted to dishonor God in their hearts.]
What did God say about Job?
    [God said Job was a perfectly upright man.]
*What did Satan think was the reason Job feared God and avoided all evil?
    [Satan thought Job feared God because God had made him rich.]
What did Satan think would cause Job to turn against God?
    [Satan thought Job would curse God if he lost his riches.]
*Who took Job's blessings away?
    [Satan took Job's blessings away.]
Was Satan right about what Job would do?
    [No, Satan was wrong.]
What did Job do when he lost his blessings?
    [Job worshiped God.]
Tell what happened on Job's day of disaster.
    [1. Sabeans stole his oxen and donkeys and killed the servants who cared for them. 2. Fire from heaven burned up his sheep and the servants who cared for them. 3. Chaldeans took his camels and killed the servants who cared for them. 4. A great wind destroyed the house his children were in and killed them all.]
What did Satan say about Job after that?
    [Satan said, "A man will give anything for his life."]
*Was Satan then saying that Job served God because God let him live instead of because God had given him blessings?
    [Satan had been proven wrong in his first accusation, so he said this. But if men serve God just because He has given them life, all men would have been as righteous as Job. Job was not serving God just because he was alive. There was something different about Job as compared with other men.]

What did Satan do next to try to get Job to curse God?

[He smote Job with severe sickness and sore boils.]

Did Satan's plan work?

[No, Job was willing to accept trouble as well as blessings.]

Workbook Note

Exercise B

Having the children write definitions from a standard dictionary may result in answers of varying meanings. You may count them correct, but it would be valuable to discuss differences of definition. Have the students recall the use of the word in the story and identify the best definition for that usage.

ANSWER KEY

A. 1. (uz) A land of the Middle East between Damascus and Edom
2. (jōb) A man from the land of Uz who suffered many trials
3. (sa•bē' ənz) People from a land to the south of Uz
4. (kal•dē' ənz) People from the land of Chaldea, near Mesopotamia and east of Uz

B. (Possible answers)
1. Keep away from
2. Property; thing owned
3. Make fun; mock
4. Event that causes much suffering or loss
5. A piece of something broken

C. 1. e
2. d
3. c
4. g
5. a
6. f
7. b
8. i
9. k
10. o
11. n
12. j
13. h
14. l
15. m

D. 3
1
5
2
4
6

E. 1. evil
2. sons, daughters
3. sacrifices
4. God
5. tore, shaved
6. Blessed
7. boils
8. trouble

F. 1. b 3. b
2. a 4. c

LESSON 2
Job's Friends Come to Visit

Oral Reading
Give realistic expression to the questions, accusations, and lamentations spoken in this lesson.

Discussion
Who were Job's three friends?
[Eliphaz, Bildad, and Zophar were Job's friends.]
What did they do in response to Job's troubles?
[They came to mourn with Job and comfort him.]
What did Job's friends do to show their grief?
[They tore their clothes and put dust on their heads.]
How long did they sit without speaking?
[They said nothing for seven days.]
*Why do you think they waited so long to talk if they came to comfort Job?
[Their grief was so great for Job's suffering.]
Who spoke first?
[Job spoke first.]
 Did Eliphaz think such things could happen to an innocent or righteous man?
[No, he thought there must be wickedness in Job's life.]
*Why did these troubles come upon Job?
[These things really happened because Job would not sin.]
*What is the answer to Bildad's question, "Is God ever unfair?"
[No, God is never unfair. But God is so much greater than what man can think, that men cannot understand His ways. Sometimes things do not look fair, but that is only because human minds are too little to see things the way God sees them.]
What did Job say would happen if he tried to prove to God that he was pure?
[Job's own words would condemn him.]
Did he try to blame God for being unfair?
[No, he said, "We cannot blame the Almighty or question what He does."]
What did Zophar call Job's words?
[Zophar accused Job of a multitude of words and lies and mocking.]
What did Zophar use for comparison when he tried to describe God's greatness?
[Zophar mentioned heaven, hell, the earth, and the sea to describe God's greatness.]
*What did Job mean when he said, "It would be wise for you to hold your peace"?
[To hold one's peace is to keep silent.]
*Why did Job wish he was in the grave?
[He was suffering greatly. He had a clear conscience before God, and he knew there would be peace for him after death.]

ANSWER KEY

A. (Order interchangeable)
1. Eliphaz (el' i•faz)
2. Bildad (bil' dad)
3. Zophar (zō' fər)

B.
1. mourn, comfort
2. recognize
3. grieved
4. innocent
5. discern
6. multitude
7. wickedness
8. slays

C. (Possible answers)
1. Job's friends came to *mourn* with him and *comfort* him.
2. They did not recognize him because Job's sickness and suffering made him *look so different*.

3. They were silent because of their great *grief*.
4. Eliphaz thought there was *sin in Job's life*.
5. God said Job was a *perfectly upright* man.

D.
1. yes   6. no
2. no   7. no
3. no   8. yes
4. yes   9. no
5. yes   10. yes

E.
1. e   5. g
2. c   6. b
3. d   7. f
4. a

LESSON 3
Discussion With Job

Oral Reading
    Read with expression suited to Job's frustration.

Discussion
*What did Eliphaz mean when he said, "You fill yourself with wind"?
    [He was accusing Job of saying many useless words. A "windy" person is a wordy talker.]
What did Eliphaz say about the mighy heavens as compared to God?
    [Even the mighty heavens are not pure in comparison to Him. (The heavens are much greater than man, but even they are nothing to be compared with God.)]
*Why did Job call his friends miserable comforters?
    [They wanted to comfort him, but they were only making him more miserable.]
*Why do you think Job wanted to plead with God?
    [Perhaps he wanted to beg for mercy. He could not understand why he should deserve all this trouble.]

Whom did Job feel had forsaken him?

[Job felt forsaken by his relatives, his friends, his servants, and his wife.]

What did Job believe about his Redeemer?

[He knew that He lives and would stand on the earth.]

What did Zophar say happens to a hypocrite?

[A hypocrite will be turned to destruction. Heaven and earth will expose his iniquity.]

Why did Job say to his friends, "Put your hand over your mouth"?

[He wanted them to stop talking because the things they said about him were false.]

*When does a person's heart reproach him?

[The voice of a guilty conscience is a person's heart reproaching him.]

Who honored and respected Job in the past days?

[The aged and the princes and nobles honored and respected Job for his wisdom.]

Who made jokes of Job and abhorred him in his troubles?

[Men of poor character and people younger than he laughed at Job.]

ANSWER KEY

A. (Possible answers)
1. A feeling of contempt
2. Beg; ask earnestly
3. Coarse, dirty, rude creatures; animals
4. A person who pretends to be good

B.
1. responded
2. unprofitable
3. vile
4. snares
5. vex
6. graven
7. triumph
8. expose
9. accuse
10. convince
11. prosperous
12. abhor
13. wealth

C.
1. a   4. c
2. b   5. c
3. a   6. b

D.
1. Eliphaz
2. miserable comforters
3. Bildad
4. his relatives, his friends, his servants, his wife
5. just for a moment
6. from God
7. the aged
8. people younger than he

Gradebook: 34 points

LESSON 4
Elihu Speaks and God Speaks

Oral Reading

Review dividing sentences into phrase units. Practice with these sentences.

God is greater than man, and He does not need to give any reason for the things He does.

Job felt very, very small and unworthy when he thought of these things.

Discussion

Why had Elihu not spoken before?

[Elihu was younger, and he kept silence out of respect to the older men and their wisdom.]

Why did Elihu speak when he did?

[He was stirred up because Job justified himself instead of glorifying God, and because the other men condemned Job without answering his questions.]

*Why is it not proper to say to a king, "You are wicked," or to say to princes, "You are ungodly"?

[Rulers should be respected simply because of their position of authority.]

What did Elihu think would be a proper response from Job?

["I have been punished; I do not want to sin any more. If I have sinned, teach me what I do not realize, and I will sin no more."]

*Does it make any difference to God whether man is righteous or wicked?

[Man's condition does not help or hinder God's position. But it does make a difference to Him in that He cares about man's experience because He loves man.]

What questions did God ask that Job could answer with no?

["Have you ever commanded the morning to come? Have you searched the depth of the sea?" *There are twenty-one such questions in the lesson.*]

*What does it mean to give counsel without knowledge?

[Giving counsel without knowledge means trying to give advice when one does not know anything about the situation.]

*Who was giving counsel without knowledge?

[This probably applies to Job and every one of his friends. None of them had knowledge enough to criticize or instruct God.]

Extra Activity

This lesson could be the basis for a profitable research project. Assign each child an animal mentioned in the passage of God's questions. Have him copy the question from the reader or from the Bible (Job 38:39–39:30), then write any information of interest on that animal found in the encyclopedia or Bible dictionary.

The project could constitute the reading assignment and class for one day. Have the reports read orally and discuss them. Express wonder at the awesome wisdom of God in all these details—not to mention the realms of the sea, the heavens, the weather, and the earth's foundation.

Workbook Note

If star pictures are completely new to your pupils, it would be advisable to discuss with them the constellations shown in number 5 of part D.

ANSWER KEY

A. (Symbols may vary slightly with dictionaries.)
1. (ō•pin' yən)
2. (kom•prē•hend')
3. (prā)
4. (ē•lī' hū)
5. (plē' ə•dēz)
6. (ô•rī' ən)
7. (maz' ə•roth)
8. (ärk•toor' əs)

B.
1. b
2. d
3. a
4. g
5. f
6. i
7. j
8. e
9. h
10. c

C.
1. c
2. e
3. b
4. g
5. a
6. d
7. f
8. j
9. i
10. h

D.
1. (drops of water)
   clouds
   lightning
   thunder
   snow
   frost
   south wind
2. lions   peacock
   ravens   ostrich
   wild goats   horse
   wild ass   hawk
   wild ox   eagle

3. a. the foundations
   b. the measure
   c. the line
   d. foundation
   e. the cornerstone
4. Pleiades
   Orion
   Mazzaroth
   Arcturus
5. a. Pleiades
   b. Arcturus
   c. Orion
   d. Mazzaroth

E.
1. a. Elihu was stirred up because *Job justified himself.*
   b. He was angry because *Job's friends had condemned Job without being able to answer his questions.*
2. Elihu thought the other men would be wiser because *they were older.*
3. *Man* is affected by wickedness or righteousness.
4. Elihu's *heart trembled* at the mighty greatness of God.
5. Job felt *very, very small and unworthy* after God talked to him.

LESSON 5
God Corrects and Blesses

Oral Reading
Encourage the children to read smoothly with meaningful phrases.

Quiz
Test comprehension and memory with an oral quiz. Have the children number their papers from 1–12 and write *true* or *false* for each of these statements.

(true)   1. God spoke to Job from a whirlwind.
(false)   2. Job could tread down the wicked and punish them.
(false)   3. Job could control the powerful behemoth.
(false)   4. A leviathan can be gentled to be a servant.
(true)   5. Everything under heaven belongs to God.
(false)   6. Eliphaz said, "I repent in dust and ashes."
(false)   7. God told Job's friends to offer ten bullocks and ten rams for an offering.
(true)   8. Job prayed for his three friends.
(false)   9. Job got all the sheep, camels, and oxen back that he had lost.
(true) 10. All Job's brothers and sisters and friends gave him money.
(true) 11. Job had another family of seven sons and three daughters.
(false) 12. Job died when he was one hundred forty years old.

Discussion
Why was God angry with Job's three friends?
   [They had not spoken things that were right.]
*What had been spoken that was not right?
   [Job's friends had strongly implied that there was sin in Job's life, which was a wrong accusation. They insisted that God would prosper Job if he were innocent, but God allows trials to the righteous.]
*The Book of Job does not say anything more about Satan talking to God. What do you think God would have said to Satan if Satan came before Him again?
   [God would probably have said, "Have you considered Job? He is a perfectly upright man who fears God and avoids evil."]

ANSWER KEY

A.
1. c	8. b	15. b	18. c
2. a	9. d	16. a	19. a
3. b	10. a	17. c	20. b
4. a	11. c		
5. c	12. a		
6. b	13. c		
7. d	14. b		

B. (Possible answers)
   1. Kill and cut up an animal for food

2. Ox; steer
3. Past; of earlier times
4. Past form of *bear*; did endure or suffer

C. (Phrases to be crossed out)

3.	11.
5.	13.
8.	15.
9.	19.
	20.

D.
1. behemoth
2. behemoth
3. leviathan
4. behemoth
5. leviathan
6. behemoth
7. leviathan
8. leviathan
9. behemoth

10. leviathan
11. behemoth
12. behemoth
13. leviathan
14. leviathan
15. behemoth

E. 1. God was angry because *they had not spoken right things.*
2. *Job's prayer* saved his friends from punishment.
3. fourteen
4. two
5. two thousand
6. fourteen thousand
7. six thousand
8. one thousand
9. twenty-three thousand
10. ten

LESSON 6
The Book of Nature and Scripture

Oral Reading

Poetry often breaks reading into phrases for us. Poetry also has accented syllables arranged in a pattern that creates a rhythm that is easy to read. Emphasizing the rhythm of accent, and lines as phrases could lead to singsong poetry reading, but use this as a beginning. Other aspects will be considered in following lessons to improve expression.

Discussion

What does the book of nature say?

[The book of nature tells of the glory of God and His handiwork.]

*How is the book understood if it never uses speech or language?

[The display of the skies and the journey of the sun give evidence of God's greatness.]

How far is the message of the heavens spread?

[The message extends through all the earth and to earth's remotest ends.]

What is compared to a man of strength and a bridegroom.

[The sun is compared to a man of strength and a bridegroom.]

*How is the sun like a man of strength?

[His brightness gives the impression of cheer as he begins his long

journey across the sky. A strong man rejoices in a long race.]
*How is the sun like a bridegroom?
[In Bible times a bridegroom would dress up with great riches and glory.
The sun is very bright and glorious.]
From where does the sun go forth each day?
[His going forth is from the end of heaven.]
How far does the circuit of the sun reach?
[His circuit reaches to the ends of the firmament.]
What is a circuit?
[A circuit is a circular route.]
What are some different names used to refer to the book of Scripture?
[The book of Scripture is called the law, testimony, statutes, precepts,
and judgments.]
The book of nature reveals God's glory. What does the book of Scripture do?
[The book of Scripture converts the soul, makes the simple wise, delights
the heart, and imparts light.]
How precious is the book of Scripture?
[It is to be desired more than finest gold, and it is sweeter than honey.]

ANSWER KEY

A. 1. e 5. g
2. d 6. b
3. a 7. h
4. f 8. c

B. 1. declare 6. converts
2. firmament 7. impart
3. utter 8. endure
4. extends 9. gold
5. chamber 10. guard

C. commandment

D. 1. show 5. pronounce
2. display 6. speak
3. flaunt 7. utter
4. reveal 8. declare

E.
2. lan' guage
3. nev' er
4. ex tends'
5. re mote'
6. cir' cuit
7. re joic' ing

8. bride' groom
9. ar ray'
10. cham' ber
11. per' fect
12. con verts'
13. tes' ti mo ny
14. sim' ple
15. stat' ute
16. de light'
17. pre' cepts
18. im part'
19. en dure'
20. judg' ments
21. ser' vant

F. 1. c 4. c
2. a 5. a
3. b 6. b

G. 1. The law of the Lord is
perfect, converting the
soul.
2. The testimony of the Lord
is sure, making wise the
simple.

3. The statutes of the Lord are right, rejoicing the heart.
4. The commandment of the Lord is pure, enlightening the eyes.
5. The fear of the Lord is clean, enduring for ever.
6. The judgments of the Lord are true and righteous altogether.

LESSON 7
The All-Seeing God

Oral Reading

The rhythm of poetry provides accent, but if that is the only voice inflection, the reading will not be very meaningful. Encourage the children to think of the meaning of the lines they read and use their voices to express the meaning.

Use an awed or impressed tone for the line, "Such knowledge is so *high,* so *grand.*"

Make the questions in stanza 4 sound like questions.

Exclaim the exclamation in stanza 5.

The line, "And dwell in utmost parts of sea," can give the impression of distance and remoteness by prolonging the vowel sounds in the syllables of *utmost.*

Discussion

Can any secrets be hidden inside a person that God does not know?
  [No, God beholds the secret thoughts.]
Is there any place a person could go to get away from God?
  [No, God is present everywhere.]
Where did the psalmist think of going when he thought of trying to get away from God?
  [He thought of heaven, the grave, utmost parts of sea, and shades of darkness as places to escape God.]
*What is the wonderful and fearful way that God has formed man's earthly frame?
  [Man's physical being is a wonder. The more one studies the muscles, bones, nerves, blood, and the way these systems all work together, the more he marvels.]
How many thoughts does God have toward His people?
  [His thoughts are more than the sand of the sea, which cannot be counted.]
*Who are men of blood?
  [Men of blood are men who shed blood—murderers.]
How did the psalmist feel toward ungodly men?
  [He did not want to be with them. It gave him grief to hear their unholy words.]

ANSWER KEY

A.
1. ascend
2. utmost
3. lo
4. survey
5. tread
6. profane
7. afar
8. shun
9. constant
10. whither
11. attend
12. presence

B.

1. b	16. a
2. c	17. b
3. a	18. a
4. a	19. b
5. b	20. a
6. a	21. a
7. c	22. c
8. c	23. b
9. a	24. a
10. b	25. a
11. a	26. a
12. b	27. b
13. a	28. b
14. b	29. b
15. c	30. a

C. I praise Thy skill when I sur-vey

The won-der-ful and fear-ful way

That Thou hast formed my earth-ly frame.

'Twas from Thy hand, my God, I came.

How pre-cious are Thy thoughts of me,

In num-ber more than sand of sea!

How faith-ful is Thy con-stant care,

When I a-wake Thou still art there.

D.
1. searching
2. mighty
3. great
4. morning
5. utmost
6. right (or) Thy
7. noonday
8. earthly
9. constant
10. holy

E.
1. a. God knew his *rising up*.
   b. God knew his *sitting down*.
   c. God knew his *thoughts*.
   d. God knew the *path* he trod.
   e. God knew his *lying down*.
   f. God knew *all his ways*.
   g. God knew the *words* in his tongue.
2. a. heaven
   b. the grave
   c. the utmost parts of the sea
   d. in shades of darkness
3. He praised God when he saw *how wonderfully God had made him*.

4. I will praise thee; for I am fearfully and wonderfully made: marvellous are thy works; and that my soul

knoweth right well.

5. He grieved when he heard people take *God's Name in vain.*

LESSON 8
The Good Shepherd

Oral Reading

Encourage expressive reading. Let the rhythm of accent be secondary to emphasis on syllables for meaning.

> The *Lord* my shepherd *feeds* me
> And I no *want* shall know;
>
> He doth, when *ill* betides me,
> Re*store* me from distress;
>
> When passing *death's dark vale;*
> My cup of *bliss* o'erflows.

Discussion

Your students may know Psalm 23 by memory. Let them recite the Psalm. Read a line or couplet from the poem and have the children give the corresponding words from the Psalm. Then ask them to also give the same thought in their own wording.

Workbook Note

A practical help for doing part D would be to mark the accent pattern for the given words, to determine the number of syllables and the accent for each blank.

Extra Activity

Memorize the poem in this lesson.

ANSWER KEY

A.				**B.** (Probable definitions)
1. d	5. b	9. k		
2. a	6. i	10. l		1. Desire; wish for
3. e	7. h	11. g		2. Sick; not healthy
4. c	8. f	12. j		

C. And I no want shall know;   6

In pas-tures green He leads me,   7

By streams which gent-ly flow.   6

He doth, when ill be-tides me,   7

Re-store me from dis-tress;   6

For His Name's sake He guides me   7

In paths of right-eous-ness.   6

D.
1. hunger
2. feedeth
3. waters
4. pass
5. not
6. valley
7. suffer
8. oil
9. richly
10. presence
11. blessing

E.
1. And I no want shall know;
2. He doth, when ill betides me, Restore me from distress;
3. And I shall fear no ill.
4. Thy rod and staff shall cheer me,
5. With oil Thou dost anoint me;
6. Until God's house receive me, Forever to abide.

F.
1. 1
2. 3
3. 4
4. 2

G.
1. The Shepherd guides him in paths of *righteousness.*
2. He guides in paths of righteousness *for the sake of His Name.*
3. The Shepherd's *rod and staff* cheer him.
4. He expected to have goodness and mercy *as long as he lived.*

H. (Individual work)

Gradebook: 54 points, counting two points for each line in part C

LESSON 9
The Works of God

Oral Reading

Remind the class that observing phrases lends smoothness to reading. Poetry lines do not necessarily constitute thought units. The following pairs of lines should be read without a break at the end of the first line because of the continued thought. Observe punctuation as a guide for pauses.

Adorned with glorious rays
Of honor, light, and majesty,

He rides on chariot clouds, and walks
On wings of wind that fly.

God sets the moon on high to mark
The seasons as they go;

He brings the darkness, when the beasts
Of forest creep abroad.

Stanza 6 is one sentence with the skeleton in lines one and four. The stanza should be read in a way that keeps the thought of the sentence clear.

Discussion

To whom is the poet talking in the first sentence in stanza 1?
[He is talking to his soul.]
To whom is he talking in the rest of stanza 1?
[He is addressing God.]
Is he talking to God in stanzas 2 through 10?
[God is referred to as *He*, so the poet is again addressing his soul, or speaking to a third person.]
Who is addressed in stanza 11?
[The words are addressed to the Lord.]
What reason is given in stanza 1 to bless and praise the Lord?
[God is worthy of blessing and praise because of His glorious honor, light, and majesty.]
*What impression of God is given by stanzas 2 and 3?
[He is immense beyond man's scope of greatness.]
*What do stanzas 4 through 10 teach us about God?
[He is kind and faithful in providing for the needs of all creatures and controlling the things He has made.]
Do conies have wings?
[No, *fly* is used in stanza 7 with the definition "run away; flee."]
How do the lions get their meat from God?
[He provided animals that the lions hunt for food.]

Workbook Note

The 8, 6, 8, 6 syllable pattern found in part C is a common meter used in songs. Some familiar songs with the 8, 6, 8, 6 meter are listed below. This poem could be sung to any of these tunes.

Alas, and Did My Saviour Bleed
Am I a Soldier of the Cross?
Amazing Grace
By Cool Siloam's Shady Rill
God Moves in a Mysterious Way
How Sweet, How Heavenly Is the Sight
I Owe the Lord a Morning Song
Jesus, the Very Thought of Thee
Oh, For a Heart to Praise My God
Thou Art the Way

ANSWER KEY

A.
1. chariot
2. herbs
3. refuge
4. fowls
5. adorned
6. clothed
7. bound
8. brink
9. cony
10. curtain
11. abroad
12. cedars

13. beam
14. manifold
15. quest
16. stately

B. 1. know, no
2. pray, prey
3. meat, meet

4. raise, rays
5. their, there
6. great, grate
7. made, maid
8. four, for
9. seize, seas
10. prays, praise

   C. The don-keys wild, and beasts of fields   8

       Come to the springs to drink.   6

    The fowls of heav-en sing God's praise   8

       In trees a-long their brink.   6

    The hills are wa-tered by the streams;   8

       The earth is sat-is-fied;   6

   And grass comes forth for cat-tle's need.   8

       With herbs man is sup-plied.   6

D. 1. donkeys, beasts
2. fowls
3. hills, earth
4. cattle, man
5. birds
6. goats, conies
7. the moon
8. beasts, lions

3. curtain
4. rides, chariot
5. walks, wings
6. foundations
7. clothed
8. bound

E. 1. adorned
2. beams

F. O Lord, how manifold are thy works! in wisdom hast thou made them all: the earth is full of thy riches.

LESSON 10
God's Goodness

Oral Reading

Evaluate the volume in oral reading. If the students need help to read more loudly, let various ones of them stand at a distance and say when the reading can be heard well.

This poem has an 8, 8, 8, 8 meter and can be sung to any of these tunes.
Before Jehovah's Awful Throne
Faith Is a Living Power From Heaven
From Every Stormy Wind That Blows
Go Labor On
Just As I Am
Lord, Speak to Me
Lord, Thou Hast Searched
Praise God From Whom All Blessings Flow
Tis Midnight, and on Olive's Brow
When I Survey the Wondrous Cross

Discussion

What does the Lord do for longing and hungry souls?
[He satisfies and fills them.]
What did the Lord do for bound rebels when they cried to Him?
[He saved them, broke their bands, and gave them light.]
What does God do for afflicted fools when they cry to Him?
[He hears, heals, and saves them.]
What does God do for distressed sailors when they cry to Him in a storm?
[He stills the waves, calms the sea, and brings them to port.]
What should men do because of these works of God?
[Men should praise the Lord for His goodness and wonderful works.]
*Which of the troubles described happen to people because of their own doing?
[Those bound in chains are in distress because they rebelled. Fools are afflicted because of their sin.]
Which word in each of these pairs gives the sadder feeling?

[longing]—satisfies   saved—[distress]
praise—[afflicted]   goodness—[sick]
rejoice—[stagger]   [raging]—exalt
[toss]—sing   [storm]—thanks

ANSWER KEY

A. 1. hungry   11. calms
2. fastened   12. deeds
3. trouble   13. praise
4. fear   14. gathered
5. wickedness   15. cry
6. ill
7. boats   **B.** 1. c   4. d
8. seas   2. e   5. f
9. throw   3. a   6. b
10. wild
C. (Individual sentences)

D. 1. a. The longing soul He *sat-isfies* / And *fills* the hungry soul that cries.

b. He *saved them* from distress and fright, / He *broke their bands* and *gave them light.*

c. He *cut the iron bars* in two, / And all the *gates* of brass *broke* through.

d. But when they cry to God *He hears* / And *heals* and *saves* them from their fears.

2. a. *Give thanks* and *offer sacrifice*; / *Rejoice* in works beyond all price.

b. *Exalt Him* in assembled crowd, / *Give praise* and *sing* and *shout* aloud!

E. longing   distress
afflicted   hungry
fears   sick
drunk   storms
dark   chains

cries   fright
bound   death
sin   stagger
raging   pains

F. 5, 8

G. 1. Lord, record
satisfies, cries
2. chains, pains
fright, light
3. Lord, record
two, through
4. sin, within
hears, fears
5. Lord, record
sacrifice, price
6. deep, leap
blow, fro
7. distress, less
sea, be
8. Lord, record
crowd, aloud

Gradebook: 85 points

LESSON 11
God's Word

Oral Reading

Remind the students to read loudly enough to be clearly heard. Require re-reading if you are not satisfied with the volume.

This poem may be sung to any tune with an 8, 6, 8, 6 meter.

Discussion

*What blessing do those have who are undefiled in heart and who keep God's Word?

[Some of the blessings mentioned in the poem are—

A warning to not turn from God,

Sweet meditation and joy,

Sweet rest and peace of mind,

A guide day and night.]

*How does a person serve God with his hands?
    [A person serves God with his hands when he uses his hands to do things
    that God wants him to do.]
What will cleanse a young man's way?
    [Taking heed to God's Word will cleanse his way.]
*How can a person hide God's Word in his heart?
    [One can hide God's Word in his heart by memorizing it and loving what
    it says.]
*What do you think could be some of the wondrous things to be seen in
God's Word?
    [Some wondrous things would be accounts of miracles. The children may
    name particular ones, or some promises.]

Workbook Notes

In part B, help the children to see the relationship between the words.
Each sentence could be reworded to express the relationship.

Fast *means the opposite of* slow and old *means the opposite of* ___.
Happy *means the same as* glad and walk *means the same as* ___.
Invite *is a root word of* invitation . . .
Joy *rhymes with* toy . . .
An apple *has a* core . . .

For part C it may be helpful to print a stanza of poetry on the chalkboard for a sample of marking the rhyme scheme.

ANSWER KEY

A. (Probable definitions)
    1. Pure; not defiled
    2. Go away; leave
    3. Make clean; purify
    4. Pay attention to; notice
    5. Looked for; tried to find
    6. Think seriously; ponder

B. 1. young
    2. blest
    3. wondrous
    4. tread
    5. cleave
    6. guide
    7. meditation
    8. warn
    9. guard
    10. heart

C. 1. a, b, a, b
    2. a, b, a, b
    3. a, b, a, b

D. (Order interchangeable)
    1. law
    2. precepts
    3. Word
    4. commands
    5. statutes

E. blest   right
    kindly   love
    rest
             clean   delight
             joy   heavenly
             wondrous   sweet
             peace

F. 1. A young man can cleanse his way *by taking heed to what God says.*
   2. *God's Word* within the heart can warn a person.

3. *God's Word* is like the sun and like a lamp.

G. 1. b   3. a
    2. a   4. c

LESSON 12
Praise

Oral Reading

Is it natural to say *ev'ry* and *glor-yus*? For the sake of rhythm these are said as two-syllable words in the poem for Psalm 145, but they are properly pronounced as three-syllable words.

Pay attention to clear pronunciation of all syllables, especially in the multisyllable words. You may want to list some of these words on the chalkboard for practice.

| evermore | mighty | greatly | unsearchable |
| majesty | greatness | forever | bestows |

Discussion

Psalm 145

What is the meaning of the lines, "Upon Thy glorious majesty / And honor I will dwell"?

[It means, "I will dwell on (think about) Thy majesty and honor."]

*What could be some of God's grand and glorious works that the poet will tell?

[He could tell of creation, seasonal changes, day and night, miracles, constant care and provision for the world of nature and for people . . .]

*What are some of God's works on which He bestows His tender love and mercy?

[All creatures are part of God's works, and all depend on His care. (Any animals or other parts of nature could be named as well as people.)]

Psalm 100

*What are the tongues of the nations?

[Tongues are languages. Many nations have different languages.]

What does *divine employ* mean?

[Divine employ is holy work or activity.]

What divine employ is mentioned in the poem?

[Paying thanks and honors in God's courts is divine employ.]

What is the whole race of man?

[The race of man is all human beings.]

Workbook Note

Review the method of marking the rhyme scheme for a stanza of poetry.

Extra Activity

Choose one of the poems in this lesson and memorize it.

ANSWER KEY

A.
1. repair
2. employ
3. unsearchable
4. race
5. extol
6. endure
7. divine
8. sovereign
9. bestows
10. court

B.
1. d
2. e
3. a
4. g
5. c
6. i
7. j
8. b
9. h
10. f

C.
1. mighty
2. greatly (or) greatness
3. greatness (or) greatly
4. glorious
5. unsearchable
6. blessing
7. cheerful
8. being
9. courts
10. truth

D. 1. The Lord our God is good to all,   8   a

From Him all bless-ing flows;   6   b

On all His works His ten-der love   8   c

And mer-cy He be-stows.   6   b

2. The Lord is good, the Lord is kind;   8   a

Great is His grace, His mer-cy sure;   8   b

And the whole race of man shall find   8   a

His truth from age to age en-dure.   8   b

E.
1. God
2. King
3. praises
4. majesty, honor
5. works, greatness

F.
1. Psalm 145
2. Psalm 100
3. Psalm 100
4. Psalm 145
5. Psalm 100

G. (Possible answers)
1. God made the earth. He divided the Red Sea for Israel. He brought water from a rock. He made the walls of Jericho fall . . .
2. The Lord bestows tender love and mercy on all people, as well as on horses, lions, bears, dogs, cats, fish, birds . . .

LESSON 13
A Prayer in Danger

Oral Reading
Try having the class read in unison.

Discussion
*What word picture is the poet thinking of when he speaks of refuge beneath God's wings?
  [A hen protects her young by hiding them under her wings.]
Who brings all things to pass for the poet?
  [God supreme brings all things to pass for him.]
What does that mean?
  [Everything that happens in his life is controlled by God.]
What word pictures does he use to describe his enemies?
  [He compares his enemies to lions with teeth like spears and hatred like fire.]
*How could the psalmist lie down and relax enough to sleep in such danger?
  [He had confidence in God's help.]
*How could he sing and give praise while he was still in danger?
  [His trust was so sure that it was just as good as if deliverance had already been accomplished.]
Pick out some words in the poem that carry a feeling of sadness or danger.
  (See Answer Key, part D below.)
Pick out some words that carry a feeling of joy and safety.
  (See Answer Key, part E below.)

Workbook Note
For part F, be sure the children use the King James Version of the Bible so that their answers match the wording of the answer key.

ANSWER KEY

A.
1. supreme
2. afford
3. downfall
4. overpast
5. prepared
6. exalted
7. blast
8. pursue
9. doom

B.
1. e
2. a
3. g
4. b
5. j
6. c
7. f
8. i
9. d
10. h

C.
8 a
8 b
8 a
8 b

D. (Any ten)

woes	hate
blast	foes
cry	pursue
dangers	lonely
fierce	catch
teeth	fall
spears	doom
fire	downfall

E. (Any ten)

Lord	heaven
merciful	praise
care	glorify
refuge	wondrous
safe	fixed
help	song
exalted	mercy
God	truths

F. 1. until these calamities be overpast
   2. in the shadow of thy wings will I make my refuge
   3. God that performeth all things for me

4. He shall send from heaven, and save me
5. For thy mercy is great unto the heavens

G. 1. 4
   2. 5, 11
   3. 6
   4. 7, 8

H. 1. three thousand
   2. David
   3. David cut off the skirt of Saul's robe.
   4. Saul
   5. Saul was the Lord's anointed.

LESSON 14
Pleading for Pardon

Oral Reading

   Practice reading in unison. You could let the boys read one verse and the girls read the next.

Discussion

Why could the psalmist hope that the Lord would be merciful to him?
   [The Lord has great lovingkindness and compassion.]
*Why did the psalmist say, "Sprinkle me with hyssop"?
   [In the Old Testament hyssop was used to sprinkle blood in special ceremonies (Exodus 12:22; Leviticus 14:6, 7, 51).]
What kind of person was the psalmist by natural birth?
   [He was sinful by birth.]
How could he have a clean heart?
   [God would create a clean heart in him.]
What would the psalmist do when he was restored?
   [He would teach transgressors God's ways and sing aloud of God.]
*What sacrifice would the psalmist give?
   [He would give the sacrifice of a broken and a contrite heart.]

Workbook Note

   The King James Version should be used to avoid confusion in filling the blanks in part F.

ANSWER KEY

	synonym	*antonym*
A.	1. purge	defile
	2. pity	cruelty
	3. sin	obedience
	4. sorry	stubborn
	5. throw	gather

rhyme
men's
fashion
confession
invite
last

B. (Individual sentences)

C. Hyssop is a *bushy plant*, used in Bible times for special ceremonies.

D.

1. 4	9. 2
2. 3	10. 2
3. 3	11. 3
4. 4	12. 3
5. 3	13. 3
6. 2	14. 2
7. 3	15. 2
8. 2	

E.

1. a	5. a
2. a	6. b
3. b	7. b
4. a	8. b

F.
1. Have mercy upon
2. Wash
3. Cleanse
4. Purge
5. Wash
6. Make . . . to hear
7. Create in . . . a clean heart
8. Renew a right spirit within
9. Cast . . . not away
10. Restore unto
11. Uphold
12. Deliver

G.
1. And David said unto Nathan, I have sinned against the Lord. And Nathan said unto David, The Lord also hath put away thy sin; thou shalt not die.
2. yes

LESSON 15
The Righteous and the Wicked

Oral Reading

Practice choral reading, striving for meaningful expression. Read one line to the class to show them which words to stress, and have them repeat it in unison.

Some tunes that fit the meter of this poem are listed below.

Loving Kindness
I'll Praise My Maker
Faith of Our Fathers
Jesus, Thy Boundless Love to Me

Discussion
What should a man delight in rather than wicked counsel?
   [The man is blest who delights in God's law.]
What are the characteristics of a tree by the water?
   [A tree by the water bears fruit and has green leaves.]
*If a good man is compared to a tree, what would be compared to the streams of water?
   [God's law is the stream that makes a man's life fruitful.]
*What could be compared to the fruit on the tree?
   [A man's good works could be thought of as fruit.]
What does the phrase *prosperity attend* mean?
   [Success shall go with the good man's doings.]
To what are ungodly men compared?
   [Ungodly men are compared to chaff.]
How are the ungodly like chaff?
   [They have no roots as a tree to keep them steady. They blow around easily in the winds of life.]

ANSWER KEY

A.
1. meditates
2. gently
3. plenteous
4. prosperity
5. judgment

B.
1. d
2. b
3. e
4. c
5. a
6. h
7. f
8. j
9. g
10. i

C. How blest the man that does not stray — 8 — a
Where wick-ed coun-sel tempts his feet; — 8 — b
Who stands not in the sin-ners' way, — 8 — a
And sits not in the scorn-er's seat. — 8 — b
But in God's law he takes de-light, — 8 — c
And med-i-tates both day and night. — 8 — c

D.
1. that walketh not in the counsel of the ungodly
2. nor standeth in the way of sinners
3. nor sitteth in the seat of the scornful
4. But his delight is in the law of the Lord
5. a tree planted by the rivers of water
6. bringeth forth his fruit in his season
7. his leaf also shall not whither
8. whatsoever he doeth shall prosper

9. Therefore the ungodly shall not stand in the judgment
10. nor sinners in the congregation of the righteous
11. the Lord knoweth the way of the righteous
12. but the way of the ungodly shall perish

E. 1. stray, stands, sits
   2. a tree
   3. chaff

F. (Possible answers)
   1. Chaff blows around easily and a tree by the water is firmly rooted.
   2. The fruit could be the good deeds a person does.

G. 1. satisfy
   2. opinion
   3. prey
   4. sincerely
   5. comprehend
   6. divine
   7. endure
   8. circuit
   9. contrite
   10. exalted (extol)
   11. employ
   12. pursue
   13. adorned (array)
   14. criticize
   15. transgression

LESSON 16
What a Day May Bring Forth

Oral Reading

Practice some of the conversation sentences to help the children read with realistic expression.

Quiz

Give a brief memory test with this oral quiz.
1. Who is the main character of the story? (Morris)
2. Who wanted a doll house? (Alice)
3. Who had car trouble? (Miss Himmon)
4. Who repaired the car? (Father)
5. Who offered cherries to the family? (Uncle Franks / Aunt Miriam)
6. Who was stung by bees? (Morris)
7. Who finished the cherries so that Mother could go along to the doctor? (Sheila and Lorene)
8. On what day did the main events of the story take place? (Saturday)
9. Where were the wheels Father wanted to sell? (behind the shop)
10. Where did Father and the boys look for the fourth wheel? (in the tall grass, in the pile of metal scraps, in the yard and garden)

Discussion

*What might have been included in the morning routine on Saturday?

[Breakfast, family worship, chores such as feeding pets, making beds, doing dishes]

*What was in the directory Mother offered to Miss Himmon?
   [The directory had a list of telephone numbers.]
What was Miss Himmon doing while Father fixed her car?
   [She was visiting with Mother.]
*Why did Morris keep one eye on the clock as he seeded cherries?
   [He was watching the time, hoping they might still get to the sale.]
What disturbed the bees that stung Morris?
   [The bees were disturbed when Morris lifted the wheel off their nest.]
*What were some of the good things about God's plan for that day?
   [A witness was given to Miss Himmon. The family got a good bargain in
   cherries when everybody was free to help with canning them. The bees
   did not attack when all the boys were out in the lot.]
Why should we never boast of plans for tomorrow?
   [We do not know what will happen in a day.]
Finish the proverb: Boast not thyself of to morrow . . .
   [for thou knowest not what a day may bring forth. (Proverbs 27:1)]

ANSWER KEY

A.
1. e	8. k
2. f	9. h
3. g	10. m
4. a	11. n
5. d	12. i
6. b	13. j
7. c	14. l

B. (Any fifteen)
asked	said
questioned	gushed
chorused	suggested
begged	reasoned
exclaimed	panted
faltered	added
answered	observed
murmured	instructed
	lamented

C.
1.	a. noun	b. verb
2.	a. verb	b. noun
3.	a. verb	b. noun
4.	a. noun	b. verb
5.	a. noun	b. verb
6.	a. noun	b. verb
7.	a. verb	b. noun
8.	a. verb	b. noun
9.	a. verb	b. noun
10.	a. verb	b. noun
11.	a. verb	b. noun

D. (Order interchangeable)
1. Father helped *Miss Himmon* with her *car trouble*.
2. They *could not find all the wheels* they wanted to take along.
3. They went to get *cherries* and canned them.
4. Morris had to be taken to the doctor because of his *bee stings*.

E.
Father	Alice
Mother	Peter
Morris	Sheila
Stanley	Lorene
Owen	

F.
1. b	5. a
2. b	6. c
3. a	7. b
4. c	8. a

LESSON 17
Slow to Anger

Oral Reading
    Discuss the emotions of some parts of the story and help the children read those parts expressively.

Discussion
Why did Ray choose Ebony for his horse?
    [He saw that Ebony would be a strong, spirited horse.]
Why did Sanford choose Sandy?
    [He thought Sandy was beautiful, and she was more gentle.]
How did Sanford get his colt to understand using the long rope?
    [He started again and again near Sandy's head, and backed slowly away.]
How did Ray show his colt that he meant what he said?
    [He switched Ebony in the face with a light branch.]
*What shows that Ebony did not understand what Ray was trying to get across?
    [Ebony was nervous and did not obey the commands as well as usual.]
When did Sanford treat his horse with a carrot?
    [He gave Sandy a carrot as a reward for good performance.]
When did Ray give his horse a carrot or other treat?
    [Ray used treats to coax Ebony to come to him.]
*What caused the difference in the behavior of the two colts?
    [Sandy was always treated with gentleness and patience. Ebony was sometimes handled roughly and did not trust his master.]
*Was the better training being done by the one who was slow to anger or the one who was mighty?
    [He that is slow to anger is better than the mighty.]
Finish the proverb: He that is slow to anger . . .
    [is better than the mighty; and he that ruleth his spirit than he that taketh a city. (Proverbs 16:32)]

ANSWER KEY

A.
1. colts
2. filly
3. saddle
4. halter
5. bridle
6. girth
7. corral
8. gallop

B. (Possible answers)
1. Overcome by force
2. Work together
3. An important point in progress
4. To rub with the nose
5. Relating to the body

C.

1. 2	7. 3	13. 3
2. 3	8. 3	14. 3
3. 3	9. 3	15. 4
4. 3	10. 3	16. 4
5. 3	11. 5	17. 3
6. 2	12. 1	18. 2

D. thrilled   freedom
eagerness   easier
beautiful
   praised   satisfying
   reward   affection
   wonderful   patted
       success

E. 4
2
5
1
3

F. 1. Ray grabbed a branch and *switched* Ebony in the face.

2. Sanford went back and *held the rope near to Sandy.*
3. Ray gave carrots to Ebony to *get him to come.*
4. Sanford gave carrots to *reward* Sandy for doing well.
5. Ray's horse was probably *black.*
6. Sanford's horse was probably *tan* or *yellowish brown.*

G. 1. a   3. a
2. c   4. c

Gradebook: 58 points for the whole lesson

LESSON 18
The Firstfruits

Discussion

What material did Gwen use to make her first rugs?
   [She made them from old clothes.]
What did she plan to do with the rugs she made?
   [She wanted to sell her rugs.]
What was the reason Mrs. Barwick came?
   [Mrs. Barwick came to buy eggs.]
*How could Mrs. Barwick notice that the rug was newly made?
   [A new rug does not lie as flat as a used one. The braid in the rug would look rounder than it does after it is tramped. There were probably scraps of the material lying nearby. Scissors, needle, and thread lying around would indicate that someone had just been working on a sewing project.]
For what four purposes did Gwen plan to use her money?
   [She planned to divide her money between church offerings, her parents, savings, and spending on more rug materials.]
How did she actually use her money?
   [She gave it all to the children's home.]
How did Gwen happen to receive the rolls of binding?
   [Gwen was helping Mrs. Franklin to clean her attic, and Mrs. Franklin wanted to get rid of them.]

Where did Mrs. Franklin get the binding?

[She had collected discarded rolls when she worked in a sewing factory.]

*Do you know what binding it? What craft project or any other use can you think of for something like that?

[Fabric pieces on pictures, bulletin board trim, string for pull toys, anything for which you might use string or light rope]

*Why do you think Gwen deserved the strips?

[She had been unselfish in giving her money and rug to those who were in need.]

Finish the proverb: Honour the Lord with thy substance, and with the firstfruits of all thine increase . . .

[So shall thy barns be filled with plenty, and thy presses shall burst out with new wine. (Proverbs 3:9, 10)

ANSWER KEY

A.
1. a. blended
   b. hurrah
   c. oval
   d. superior
2. a. braiding
   b. challenging
   c. sturdy
3. a. appreciate
   b. household
   c. quarters / Home
4. a. material(s)
   b. means
   c. realized
5. a. craft
   b. discarded
   c. garments
   d. tackled

B.
1. 1   7. 2   13. 2
2. 4   8. 3   14. 2
3. 4   9. 2   15. 3
4. 3   10. 2   16. 2
5. 3   11. 2   17. 3
6. 4   12. 4   18. 3

C. (The rug should be oval in shape and be colored various shades of green, gray, and brown.)

D. (These numbers should be marked with *X*.) 4, 5, 8, 9

E.
1. First she *cut strips* of material from old clothes.
2. Next she *braided* the strips.
3. Then she *stitched* the braid around and around to make an oval shape.

F.
1. c   3. a
2. b   4. d

G.
1. a   5. a
2. b   6. a
3. b   7. b
4. b

H. (Possible answers)
fine patchwork
crocheting rugs
scraps for scrapbooks
curtain ties
ties for giftwrapping
braided jump ropes
apron strings
tying up climbing roses or berry canes
binding quilts or garments

LESSON 19
Flattery's Net

Oral Reading

Use a lowered tone for Harold's thoughts, and a louder tone for his spoken words.

Discussion

What were some things that were different about the new place to which the Graysons moved?

[There were winding stairs in the house. There was no garage.]

Where did Neil keep his rabbits at their old home?

[He kept them in the garage.]

*Why do you think Neil went to find Father when he saw the boards and wire in the shed?

[He wanted to talk to Father about making rabbit pens from the boards and wire.]

*Do you think Harold was a good neighbor?

[Harold was not a good neighbor in praising Neil's pens and rabbits insincerely. He was a good neighbor in wanting to make Neil feel good.]

*How could Harold have been a better neighbor?

[He could have kindly given Neil some help to make his pens better.]

Finish the proverb: A man that flattereth his neighbour . . .

[spreadeth a net for his feet. (Proverbs 29:5)]

ANSWER KEY

A.
1. c
2. d
3. g
4. a
5. b
6. e
7. f
8. o
9. m
10. h
11. k
12. j
13. n
14. i
15. l

3. The shed did not have windows.
4. Bronco, Samantha, Hazy, Liskin, Hobo
5. Harold said the pens were so good. (Neil also wanted to save the boards to build more pens.)

B.
1. ride
2. tin cans
3. break
4. sick
5. market
6. build
7. splintered
8. pens
9. business
10. pride

C.
1. a garage
2. junk, thin boards, a roll of chicken wire

D.
1. a, c, d, f, g, h
2. He thought he could make *rabbit pens* from the boards and wire.
3. Harold gave a *friendly wave* to his new neighbor. (or) Harold *wanted to make Neil feel accepted.*
4. He said things that were *not sincere.*

E. (Possible answers)

1. "That's pretty good for the materials you have. Maybe I can help you make them stronger."

2. "I'm sure you enjoy your pets. Maybe Father could say what would be good for them."

Gradebook: 41 points

LESSON 20
Disappointed Brothers

Oral Reading

Review the aspects of oral reading as outlined on page 8. Prompt your class in any areas in which they need improvement as you cover the rest of the reader.

Discussion

*How do you know Ernest and Clarence came from a poor family?

[What they earned from wood carvings was a welcome help in providing the family's needs. They were unable to buy the new boots they needed.]

How could Ernest have gotten more carvings made?

[He could have worked at carving even if he didn't feel very much like it.]

How could Clarence have gotten more carvings made?

[He could have put more work into finishing the pieces he started instead of throwing them away.]

Why were the boys embarrassed by the skimpy size of their packs compared to Peter's?

[They were ashamed that they had not done more carvings.]

*Which of the two brothers did the better carving?

[Ernest, because he received more money for the same number of pieces.]

Could the boys have known before they left home how much money they would be paid?

[No, Mr. Karl paid according to his evaluation of skill as well as size.]

Finish the proverb: He also that is slothful in his work . . .

[is brother to him that is a great waster. (Proverbs 18:9)]

Extra Activity

Have someone do some research on Switzerland and the Alps. Locate Switzerland on a globe or world map.

ANSWER KEY

A. (Symbols may vary with dictionaries.)

1. (swis)   3. (alps)
2. (sha•lā')

B.
1. Swiss
2. franc
3. chalet
4. chisel
5. mallet
6. whittle
7. carving
8. kindling
9. hobby

C. 1. d   5. h
   2. f   6. c
   3. b   7. a
   4. e   8. g

D. 1. flattered, lamented, complimented, soothingly
   2. halter, girth, saddle, bridle
   3. mechanic, veterinarian
   4. a. abruptly
      b. fragile
      c. interruption
      d. anxious
      e. directory
      f. superior
      g. oval
      h. appreciate
      i. auction
      j. secure

E. 1. a. dog
      b. squirrel, chalet
      c. horse, cubs
   2. a. 6   b. 5   c. 12
   3. 25 francs
   4. 4 francs

F. (Possible answers)
   1. He only worked at his carving *when he felt like it.*
   2. He *threw away pieces* of wood that could have been used.
   3. They both did the *same number* of carvings.
   4. Both faults are *equally bad.*

G. 1. (Switzerland colored green)
   2. (Lake Lucerne colored blue)
   3. (Lucerne circled)

LESSON 21
Joined Hands

Discussion

Why would there be no sledding at school that day?

[Neighbor Mullen had complained about damage to his field, and Brother Eby had told the children they would need to stay inside the fence again.]

*Fifteen pupils are named in the story. Was that all the children in school?

[No, of the "handful of the youngest," only Eric is named.]

*First grade is mentioned in the story. What clues indicate that there were also upper-grade students in the school?

[The boys were big enough to help someone stuck in the snow. Lena Jane was given the responsibility for wrapping Clara's ankle.]

*Why did the recess seem long to Eric?

[The strangeness of the situation made it seem like a long time.]

*How do you know the bell rang at the normal time?

[It rang soon after Eugene gasped, "Just in time," looking at his watch as they returned to the playground.]

Does it matter how many people do something if it is wrong?

[Though hand join in hand, the wicked shall not be unpunished.]

Finish the proverb: Though hand join in hand . . .

[the wicked shall not be unpunished: but the seed of the righteous shall be delivered. (Proverbs 11:21)]

Workbook Note

You may want to assign names to your students for part F. Or you could list the names on the chalkboard as they are chosen, and ask each one to take a different name.

Extra Activity

Have students draw maps of the story setting, including all the details they can glean from the story. Maps should show schoolhouse, playground, fence, Mr. Mullen's field, plot of pines, road, Carder's pond.

Observe how diagrams can vary and still be correct.

ANSWER KEY

A.
1. her self
2. out side
3. with in
4. play ground
5. snow tag
6. snow man
7. any one
8. land scape
9. pick up
10. snow banks
11. any way
12. some one
13. every body
14. some body
15. school house
16. after noon

B.
1. bare
2. some
3. new
4. rows allowed
5. road write
6. through
7. not
8. know
9. see
10.
11.
12. so

C.
1. b
2. f
3. a
4. d
5. c
6. e
7. h
8. g

D. Clara
Barbara
Leon
Titus
Raymond
Joe
Brendon
Andrew
John
Loretta
Lena Jane
Dorothy
Mabel
Eric
Eugene

E. (Answers should contain one of the points given for each number.)

1. Suggestion to help push the pickup

   Reasoning about staying off the field

   Decision to hurry

   First one over the fence

2. Trouble keeping at English lesson

   Chosen to help make track for snowtag

   Asked what the others were doing over the fence

   Asked if Dorothy wasn't coming

   Debated but followed the others

   Slipped on a log and sprained her ankle

3. Would not go over the fence

   Played with the little children

   Got to help first graders write their sentences

4. Thought they should ask before going over the fence

Went with the second group

5. Stayed inside the fence

Thought recess was long

F. (Individual work)

G. 1. b   4. c
      2. c   5. a
      3. a   6. b

LESSON 22
Grievous Words

Discussion

Teacher: This story is based on an actual incident.

What did the Indians carry along to eat the day they picked berries?

[They carried dried venison, or jerky.]

What did they drink?

[They drank water from the river.]

How did the Delaware squaws know it was not warriors they heard in the forest?

[Warriors would make no sounds. They heard children talking.]

*Why would warriors not make any sounds in the woods if the women and children did?

[The women and children were not careful about their movements because they did not think there was any danger. Warriors, especially when on a mission of danger or attack, would move silently.]

Why did the warriors of the two tribes fight?

[Their squaws stirred them up with angry reports.]

Why did the squaws become upset with each other?

[Their children were fighting.]

Why did the children quarrel?

[They quarreled over a grasshopper.]

*Do you think anybody understood the whole situation?

[The tribes spoke different languages; probably none of the grown people understood just how foolish the whole issue was.]

Finish the proverb: A soft answer turneth away wrath . . .

[but grievous words stir up anger. (Proverbs 15:1)]

ANSWER KEY

A. 1. jerky
        2. squaws
        3. portions
        4. venison
        5. warriors

6. tribe
7. gestures (or) sign language
8. shallow
9. indignation
10. rehearsed

11. incident
12. braves
13. papooses
14. grievous
15. former

B. 1. Munhoka
2. Lenni
3. Susquehanna
4. Delaware
5. Shawnee

C. (These numbers should be marked with *G*.)

2	12	24
5	13	26
6	15	27
7	16	28
9	18	29
10	20	

D.

3	6
4	8
2	5
1	7

E. 1. blackberries, jerky (or venison)
2. bark
3. warriors
4. They used sign language.
5. There were more berries than they could gather.
6. the ground, leaves, a grasshopper

F. A soft answer turneth away wrath.

G. (Individual work)

H. 1. (Susquehanna River colored blue)
2. (Circle around river at Wilkes-Barre)
3. Chesapeake
4. (Delaware colored green)

LESSON 23
Enemies at Peace

Quiz

Read each of these sentences to the students and have them decide whether it gives a peaceful and pleasant feeling, or conveys tension and trouble. Have them number their papers to 26 and write *P* for each peaceful sentence, and *T* for each sentence of tension or trouble.

(P) 1. Peter directed the cows into the small log barn, and then he took a three-legged stool from its peg on the wall.

(T) 2. Sarah darted into the stall, her face pale beneath her freckles.

(T) 3. Peter's eyes grew round.

(P) 4. "Whatever happens, we are safe in God's hands."

(T) 5. A screech owl's eerie cry rang from the nearby woods, and Sarah jumped.

(T) 6. She was trembling when they entered the house, and her face was paler than before.

(P)   7.   There was peace in the cozy kitchen.

(P)   8.   Soft lamplight shone over the simple meal spread on the table.

(P)   9.   It cast a gentle glow on Mother's serene face.

(P) 10.   Mother did not seem at all worried.

(T) 11.   "Will you pull the latchstring inside tonight?"

(P) 12.   "We always leave the latchstring hanging out, so that all who would enter may feel welcome."

(P) 13.   Mother spoke gently, "God's love in our hearts is for all, friend or foe."

(P) 14.   They were trusting in God.

(P) 15.   Moonlight flooded the valley.

(T) 16.   Then all was quiet—too quiet, Peter thought, and again he felt uneasy.

(T) 17.   The silence of the night seemed threatening.

(T) 18.   A dozen dark figures crept stealthily through the night and surrounded the log cabin.

(P) 19.   Then not a sound could be heard except gentle snoring in the bedroom.

(T) 20.   "Peter, Peter!" Mother's voice was urgent.

(T) 21.   Suddenly he gasped and stared hard.

(T) 22.   Peter swung down the ladder and dashed into the kitchen.

(P) 23.   "The Indians left them here as a sign to us, I believe, to show us that they were here and left peaceably."

(T) 24.   "You mean the Indians were right here in our house while we were asleep?"

(P) 25.   "Come, let us kneel together and thank Him for His care."

26.   Now finish Proverbs 16:7: When a man's ways please the Lord . . . [he maketh even his enemies to be at peace with him.]

ANSWER KEY

A. (Possible answers)
1. The half light at sunset
2. Ghostly and frightening
3. Shake or tremble
4. Calm and peaceful
5. Made a ringing tone
6. Someone who enters without being asked

B.
1. by		6. light	
2. light		7. side / lines	
3. time		8. stead	
4. string		9. steps	
5. night		10. thing	

C.   1. (Any two)

He *gave the Indians corn* when their food supplies were low.

He tried to *show to the Indians the love of God.*

He always *left the latchstring out* so that anyone would feel welcome.

He had *prayer* with his family at bedtime.

2. God *moved their hearts* to leave them in peace.

D. 1. c   8. j
       2. e   9. h
       3. a   10. m
       4. f   11. k
       5. b   12. n
       6. d   13. l
       7. g   14. i

E. 1. morrow, knowest, not, day
       2. anger, mighty, ruleth, city

3. substance, firstfruits, increase, plenty
4. flattereth, net
5. slothful, brother, waster
6. join, wicked, righteous, delivered
7. soft, turneth, away, grievous, stir, up
8. please, enemies, peace

LESSON 24
The Rich Poor

Discussion

How did Timothy find his first arrowhead?
   [Arnold told him where to look.]
*How did Justin make himself rich?
   [He kept all his best arrowheads and traded to get the best ones that others found.]
*How did Arnold make himself poor?
   [He gave away his good arrowheads.]
What kind of arrowheads do you think Justin traded for Timothy's big one?
   [They must not have been very special, because Timothy seemed disgusted the next week.]
Locate Iowa and Pennsylvania on a United States map.
Finish the proverb: There is that maketh himself rich . . .
   [yet hath nothing: there is that maketh himself poor, yet hath great riches. (Proverbs 13:7)]

Extra Activity

   Have someone do some research on Indians of different areas—their homes, food, weapons, and transportation.

ANSWER KEY

A. 1. f   6. i
       2. d   7. a
       3. j   8. g
       4. b   9. h
       5. c   10. e

B. 1. 3   2. 4

C. 1. a   7. c
       2. b   8. c
       3. a   9. b
       4. b   10. a
       5. b   11. b
       6. a   12. a

D. 1. arrowheads
    2. ground
    3. Arnold
    4. two
    5. ten
    6. October
    7. chipped
    8. Arnold
    9. book / package / letter
   10. Mother

E. 1. a. R   2. a. P
    b. P   b. R
    c. P   c. P
    d. R   d. R
    e. R   e. R
    f. P   f. P
    g. R   g. R
    h. P   h. R

    3. a. Justin
       b. Arnold

Gradebook: 52 points

LESSON 25
Better Than Great Treasure

Discussion

How was mealtime different in the two homes where Julia stayed?
   [Aunt Lorraine provided food, but the family did not eat together. The Kellers all gathered around the table. The Kellers had prayer before the meal.]
How did the homes look different?
   [Aunt Lorraine's home had many pretty knickknacks; the Keller home was plain.]
How were the parents different in the two homes?
   [Aunt Lorraine did a lot of scolding, but gave in to her son. Father Keller was kind but firm.]
How were the toys different in the two homes?
   [Jeffrey had many expensive toys; the Kellers had homemade toys.]
How were the children different in the two homes?
   [Jeffrey was spoiled and unhappy; the Kellers were happy.]
If you had to choose between these two homes, where would you want to live?
Finish the proverb: Better is little with the fear of the Lord . . .
   [than great treasure and trouble therewith. (Proverbs 15:16)]

ANSWER KEY

A. 1. a. precious
      b. precocious
    2. a. refuge
      b. refulgent
    3. a. surmount
      b. surrounded

    4. a. disarray
      b. disable
    5. a. trivial
      b. triumphant
    6. a. fossil
      b. foster

7. a. agency
b. agenda
8. a. knickers
b. knickknacks
9. a. mottoes
b. mottled
10. a. blurted
b. blurry

B. 1. precious / chime
2. terrible
3. frightful
4. (more) peaceful
5. stuffed
6. electric
7. spoiled / little
8. many / extra
9. colorful
10. expensive
11. foster / new / happy
12. special

C. (Possible answers)
1. not many pretties
homemade
not new
2. very kind
Jesus in the family
live the way the Bible
teaches

3. stuffed animals and toy
trucks
new house
knickknacks
4. frightful pout
screamed
mischief

D. 1. b
2. c
3. c
4. a

E. 1. Julia was living with her
aunt because her *parents
had been killed.*
2. Jeffrey probably had a
hamburger and ice cream
for dinner.
3. The Keller house *did not
have pretty knickknacks.*
4. She thought that *her own
dolls were prettier* than
Alice's.
5. She thought *Alice was hap-
pier than Jeffrey* with all
his expensive toys.

LESSON 26
The Best Medicine

Discussion
Why was Mother sick?
[She had started coughing after the day she walked two miles in the rain.]
*Why did Mother have a broken spirit?
[She had pneumonia, her baby had died, her husband was a drunkard.]
*Why was Betsy afraid when she first saw her father?
[The last time he was home, he had been drunken and angry.]
Why was her fear replaced by wonder?
[Father looked different—his face was tender, and he had tears.]
What helped Mother recover more than the medicine the doctor had given?

[A merry heart helped her get well—gladness about her husband's conversion.]
What clue do we have that Aunt Nora was a Christian?
[She told Betsy they are praying that God would heal Mother.]
What clue do we have that Mother was a Christian?
[She whispered, "Praise God," when her husband told her he was saved.]
Finish the proverb: A merry heart doeth good like a medicine . . .
[but a broken spirit drieth the bones. (Proverbs 17:22)]

ANSWER KEY

A.
1. coughing, laughing
2. telephone
3. pneumonia
4. commotion, salvation
5. opportunity
6. forlorn

B.
1. desperate
2. telephone
3. laughed
4. commotion
5. forlorn
6. medicine
7. coughing
8. opportunity
9. huddled
10. pneumonia
11. salvation
12. rebellion

C.
1. true
2. true
3. true
4. false
5. false
6. true
7. false
8. false
9. false
10. false

11. true
12. true
13. true
14. true
15. true
16. false
17. false
18. false
19. false
20. true

D. (Sentences to be underlined)
1, 4, 5

E. (Answers should contain one of the points given for each number.)
1. He was sick and died.
2. They lived two miles away. They took Mother and the sick baby to the doctor.
3. (Many correct answers)
4. (Many correct answers)
5. (Many correct answers)
6. He came home drunk.
   He blamed Mother and Betsy for the baby's death.
   He found salvation.
   He brought Mother the best medicine.

F. Betsy

LESSON 27
Fuel for Fire

Discussion

What were some reasons the men could not get together for woodcutting?
[Mr. Mackenzie had to help his brother's family to move. Mr. Ford was called for emergency service on his job. Mr. Ford was sick.]

Was Mr. Ford disgusted about the woodcutting problem when he told Mr. Strife about it?

[No, he was just concerned that Mrs. Spencer might get worried.]

Did Mr. Strife give an honest report to Mr. Mackenzie?

[No, he said Mr. Ford was disgusted.]

*Why did the two men grow angry with each other?

[Someone was telling them unkind things about each other.]

*Do you think Mr. Ford and Mr. Mackenzie were Christians?

[We would not expect Christians to respond to a talebearer the way these men did.] *Teacher:* Emphasize this point strongly: Even though other people may be talebearers, that is no excuse for strife and ill will.

Finish the proverbs: Where no wood is . . .

[there the fire goeth out: so where there is no talebearer, the strife ceaseth.]

As coals are to burning coals, and wood to fire . . .

[so is a contentious man to kindle strife.]

The words of a talebearer are as wounds . . .

[and they go down into the innermost parts of the belly. (Proverbs 26:20–22)]

ANSWER KEY

A.
1. talebearer
2. strife
3. Ceaseth
4. contentious
5. kindle

B.
1. proposed
2. emergency
3. irritated
4. arrested (or) caught, imprisoned
5. dishonest
6. opportunity
7. cautiously

C. (Individual work)

D.
1. no
2. no
3. no
4. no
5. no
6. no
7. no

E. (Possible answers)
1. They planned to *cut her winter firewood*.
2. *Mr. Ford* told Mr. Strife about the plans.
3. It *stirred up strife* in Mr. Mackenzie.
4. He was caught in *dishonest business*.
5. There was *no talebearer* stirring up their anger.
6. They wanted to *cut wood* for Mrs. Spencer.
7. The song of the saws was the *noise the saws made*.

F.
1. The fire gets bigger.
2. The fire gets bigger.
3. The strife grows.
4. The fire goes out.
5. The strife stops.

LESSON 28
Thou Shalt Understand

Discussion

*How do you know this story happened many years ago?

[The book John Bunyan wrote has been loved and studied hundreds of
years. John Bunyan lived from 1628 to 1688.]

How did John try to find salvation at first?

[He tried to stop sinning and do good things by his own efforts.]

How was John finally saved?

[He believed in the blood of Jesus for salvation.]

Why did speaking about the Lord get John into trouble?

[It was against the law for anyone except ordained ministers to preach.]

What did John do in prison?

[He told the other prisoners about the Lord, worshiped and prayed with
them, and did some writing.]

Locate England on a globe or world map.

Finish the proverb: Yea, if thou criest after knowledge, and liftest up thy
voice for understanding . . .

[If thou seekest her as silver, and searchest for her as for hid treasures;
then shalt thou understand the fear of the Lord, and find the knowledge
of God. (Proverbs 2:3–5)]

Extra Activity

Have someone do some research on the book *Pilgrim's Progress*, or tell
the story to the children briefly.

ANSWER KEY

A.
1. seekest
2. find
3. voice
4. knowledge
5. silver
6. criest
7. hid / God / and
8. God
9. searchest
10. up
11. then
12. Lord / find
13. fear
14. after
15. shalt
16. liftest
17. treasures
18. knowledge
19. hid / God / and
20. if
21. understand
22. God

B.
1. g
2. a
3. d
4. c
5. f
6. b
7. e

C.

4	5	11	15
2	6	12	13
1	7	10	14
3	8	9	16

D. (Bedford circled)

E. 1. *John Bunyan* is the main character in this story.
2. John left school *to work* and help support the family.
3. *John's wife* started him thinking about God.
4. John was put into prison *for preaching*.

5. A book John Bunyan wrote has been loved and studied *hundreds of years*.

Gradebook: 56 points, counting two points for each sentence in part E

LESSON 29
No Lack

Discussion
Mueller can be pronounced (mū' lər), (mul' ər), or (mil' ər).
*How can one give things to God?
[He that hath pity upon the poor lendeth unto the Lord.]
*Who saw to it that there was always enough to provide for the orphans?
[God moved people to give at the right times.]
Why do you think the workers wanted to continue the boiler repairs all night?
[God put it in their hearts in answer to George's prayer.]
What are the pounds mentioned in the story?
[A pound is a British money unit, equal to one hundred new pence, or formerly twenty shillings.]
Finish the proverbs: He that giveth unto the poor . . .
[shall not lack: but he that hideth his eyes shall have many a curse. (Proverbs 28:27)]
He that hath pity upon the poor lendeth unto the Lord . . .
[and that which he hath given will he pay him again. (Proverbs 19:17)]

ANSWER KEY
A. 1. donation
2. minister
3. education
4. insane
5. gaudy
6. orphan
7. furnishings
8. boiler

B. (Order interchangeable)
1. penny(ies)
2. shilling(s)
3. pound(s)

C. (Individual work)

D. 1. *George Mueller* is the main character in this story.
2. The orphans were treated *like prisoners.* (or) They were *not given an education.*
3. In a few months George had *forty-two* orphans.
4. In two years George had *three* houses full of orphans.

5. *Five* large houses were built at Ashley Down for the orphans.
6. They *prayed* for God to give what they needed, and *people donated* gifts to them.
7. God kept His promise that they should *not lack*.
8. They gave some money to *mission work*.

E.
1. (Box around Bristol)
2. (Line from London to Bristol)
3. (Tiny house drawn at Ashley Down)
4. Avon River

F.
1. there is that maketh himself poor, yet hath great riches. (Proverbs 13:7)
2. than great treasure and trouble therewith. (Proverbs 15:16)
3. but a broken spirit drieth the bones. (Proverbs 17:22)
4. so where there is no talebearer, the strife ceaseth.
   so is a contentious man to kindle strife.
   and they go down into the innermost parts of the belly. (Proverbs 26:20–22)
5. and liftest up thy voice for understanding;
   and searchest for her as for hid treasures;
   and find the knowledge of God. (Proverbs 2:3–5
6. but he that hideth his eyes shall have many a curse. (Proverbs 28:27)
   and that which he hath given will he pay him again. (Proverbs 19:17)

LESSON 30
Diligent in His Business

Discussion

How was Booker T. Washington diligent in his business?

[He did his errand and was back in a hurry. He did his best at the salt furnace. He started work at four o'clock in the morning so that he could go to school. He attended night classes and studied as well as he could. He kept the grass cut, kept the fence in repair and painted, and was particular about trash. He walked part way, and worked to earn money, to travel to Hampton. He swept the room three times, moved the furniture, and dusted four times. He studied books as diligently as he had cleaned the classroom. He started a new school.]

*In what way did Booker stand before kings?

[Presidents and other government leaders looked to him for advice.]

How much do you value the privilege to learn? Booker was near the age of a fourth grader when he worked the four-to-nine A.M. and four-to-six P.M. hours for the privilege of going to school in between.

How old was Booker when he took the job with Mrs. Ruffner?
[He was fourteen.]
How long did he work for Mrs. Ruffner?
[He worked for Mrs. Ruffner two years.]
Locate Virginia and West Virginia on a United States map.
Finish the proverb: Seest thou a man diligent in his business? he shall
stand . . .
[before kings; he shall not stand before mean men. (Proverbs 22:29)]

Review
   Give these basic story plots and see if the children can quote a proverb
to fit each one.
   1. A family was planning to go to a sale the next day, but they never got
      there.
      [Boast not thyself of to morrow; for thou knowest not what a day may
      bring forth. (Proverbs 27:1)]
   2. Two boys were training colts, and one had better success because he
      did not become angry.
      [He that is slow to anger is better than the mighty; and he that ruleth
      his spirit than he that taketh a city. (Proverbs 16:32)]
   3. A girl gave away her first rug and the money from the first one she
      sold, and soon she got materials to make many more rugs.
      [Honour the Lord with thy substance, and with the firstfruits of all
      thine increase; so shall thy barns be filled with plenty, and thy presses
      shall burst out with new wine. (Proverbs 3:9, 10)]
   4. A boy flattered his neighbor, and that led to trouble for the neighbor.
      [A man that flattereth his neighbour spreadeth a net for his feet.
      (Proverbs 29:5)]
   5. Two boys did woodcarving for some income. One was lazy, the other
      was wasteful, and neither one was a very great success.
      [He also that is slothful in his work is brother to him that is a great
      waster. (Proverbs 18:9)]
   6. Many children thought it would be all right to disobey a school rule
      because everybody else did, but they were punished.
      [Though hand join in hand, the wicked shall not be unpunished: but
      the seed of the righteous shall be delivered. (Proverbs 11:21)]
   7. Such a small thing as a quarrel over a grasshopper grew to a battle
      between two Indian tribes.
      [A soft answer turneth away wrath: but grievous words stir up anger.
      (Proverbs 15:1)]
   8. A godly father did not resist the Indians, and they left his family in
      peace.
      [When a man's ways please the Lord, he maketh even his enemies to
      be at peace with him. (Proverbs 16:7)]

9. One boy selfishly collected the best arrowheads for himself at the expense of friendship. His brother gave away the best and gained rich blessings.
   [There is that maketh himself rich, yet hath nothing: there is that maketh himself poor, yet hath great riches. (Proverbs 13:7)]
10. A child given many toys and privileges without the love of God was not as happy as those in a poor family who loved Jesus.
   [Better is little with the fear of the Lord than great treasure and trouble therewith. (Proverbs 15:16)]
11. Glad news cheered a sick mother who seemed about to die, and she grew well rapidly.
   [A merry heart doeth good like a medicine: but a broken spirit drieth the bones. (Proverbs 17:22)]
12. An unkind man said things that made his neighbors angry with each other. When he was out of the way, the quarrel died.
   [Where no wood is, there the fire goeth out: so where there is no talebearer, the strife ceaseth. (Proverbs 26:20)]
13. A poor man sought desperately to find salvation, and he was able to help many others through his preaching and writing.
   [Yea, if thou criest after knowledge, and liftest up thy voice for understanding; if thou seekest her as silver, and searchest for her as for hid treasures; then shalt thou understand the fear of the Lord, and find the knowledge of God. (Proverbs 2:3–5)]
14. A man gave all he had for poor orphans, and he always had enough to care for them.
   [He that giveth unto the poor shall not lack: but he that hideth his eyes shall have many a curse. (Proverbs 28:27)]
15. A slave boy did everything with all his might. He became a great leader.
   [Seest thou a man diligent in his business? he shall stand before kings; he shall not stand before mean men. (Proverbs 22:29)]

ANSWER KEY

A.
1. c	6. f
2. e	7. d
3. g	8. j
4. a	9. b
5. i	10. h

8. chalet
9. girth
10. emergency
11. orphanage
12. customer
13. relic
14. forlorn
15. surplus
16. eerie

B.
1. propose
2. pneumonia
3. agency
4. shilling
5. franc
6. utensils
7. papoose

C. (Phrases to be underlined)
   1, 3, 6, 8, 9

D. 1. *Booker Washington* is the main character in this story.
2. He did his errand and was *back in a hurry*.
3. Booker *did his best* at the salt furnace.
4. He started work at *four o'clock in the morning* so that he could go to school.
5. He attended *night classes* and studied as well as he could.
6. He kept the *grass cut*, kept the *fence repaired and painted*, and was *particular about trash*.
7. He *walked* and *worked* to earn his way.
8. He *swept the room three times, moved the furniture, and dusted four times*.
9. He *studied books as diligently* as he had cleaned the classroom.
10. He started a *new school*.

E. 1. (Roanoke circled)
2. (Line from Roanoke to Malden)
3. (Dotted line from Malden to Hampton)

TEST

ANSWER KEY

A.
1. saunter
2. kindling
3. chalet
4. elastic
5. iniquity
6. firmament
7. majesty
8. expose
9. venison
10. grievous
11. serene
12. quartz
13. souvenir
14. rehearsed
15. disaster

B.

4	9	15
3	6	14
1	8	13
2	10	12
5	7	11

C.
1. Boast, day
2. anger, spirit
3. flattereth, net
4. slothful, brother
5. soft, wrath
6. enemies, peace
7. little, trouble
8. heart, medicine
9. wood, strife
10. silver, knowledge
11. poor, lack
12. diligent, kings

D.
1. A, B
2. B, A
3. A, B

Gradebook: 60 test points